1.50

Since 1969, Antonia Fraser has written many acclaimed historical works which have been international bestsellers. These include the biographies *Mary Queen of Scots* (James Tait Black Memorial Prize), *Cromwell: Our Chief of Men* and *King Charles II,* and *The Gunpowder Plot: Terror and Faith in 1605* (St Louis Literary Award; CWA Non-Fiction Gold Dagger). Four highly praised books focus on women in history: *The Weaker Vessel: Woman's Lot in Seventeenth-Century England* (Wolfson Award for History, 1984), *The Warrior Queens: Boadicea's Chariot* (1988), *The Six Wives of Henry VIII* (1992) and *Marie Antoinette: The Journey* (Enid McLeod Literary Prize, Franco-British Society, 2001). Antonia Fraser is the editor of the series *Kings and Queens of England,* (Weidenfeld & Nicolson), and wrote the volume *King James VI of Scotland, I of England.* She is married to Harold Pinter and lives in London. Antonia Fraser was made CBE in 1999, and awarded the Norton Medlicott Medal by the Historical Association in 2000. Her latest book, *Love and Louis XIV: the Women in the Life of the Sun King,* is published by Phoenix.

The Warrior Queens
Boadicea's Chariot

~

ANTONIA FRASER

Volume One

PHOENIX

This edition produced for The Book People Ltd,
Hall Wood Avenue, Haydock, St Helens WA11 9UL

First published in Great Britain in 1988
as *Boadicea's Chariot*
by George Weidenfeld & Nicolson Ltd
First published in paperback in 1993
by Mandarin Paperbacks

Paperback edition published in 2002
by Phoenix,
an imprint of Orion Books Ltd,
Orion House, 5 Upper St Martin's Lane,
London WC2H 9EA

A CIP catalogue record for this book is available from the British Library.

ISBN 978 1 4072 1647 8

Printed and bound in Great Britain by
Clays Ltd, St Ives plc

The Orion Publishing Group's policy is to use papers that are natural, renewable
and recyclable products and made from wood grown in sustainable forests. The
loggingand manufacturing processed are expected to conform to the environmental
regulations of the country of origin.

www.orionbooks.co.uk

For my eleven granddaughters

Stella, Blanche, Atalanta, Eliza, Honor,
Ana Sofia, Oriana, Phoebe, Miranda, Cecilia and Allegra

To inspire them

Contents

Author's Note

'That's the Romans for you – four hundred years of occupying *our* country': these indignant words were spoken in 1986 by one who, like myself, was gazing down from an observer's platform into some archaeological excavations in the City of London. Such robust patriotism, undaunted by the passage of quite a lot of time, reminded me of my earliest involvement with Queen Boadicea, via H. E. Marshall's inimitable *Our Island Story*, a work enjoyed by me with passion as a child in the 1930s. It was Boadicea the patriotic heroine whose story first thrilled me; I wept for her treatment – and that of her daughters – and wept again, but this time in admiration, for her death.

The word heroine, as opposed to hero, is important in all this: for there is no doubt in my mind that a part – indeed a large part – of Boadicea's appeal to me then lay in her female sex (the early feminism of those who have brothers close in age should never be underestimated). Half a century later in exploring both the history and the subsequent reputation of Queen Boadicea, those two interwoven themes of her patriotism and her femininity have not seemed to me either irrelevant or outmoded. I suppose therefore I can claim a lifetime's preoccupation with the subject of Boadicea, even if my early feelings of dislike for the misogynist Romans have waned – just a little.

In recounting the stories of other Warrior Queens, as indeed in investigating that of Boadicea herself, I have obviously been dependent on the works of many scholars and experts in their field, to which detailed acknowledgement is made in the Reference Notes, but I should like to express my deep overall gratitude here. The spelling of proper names in a book crossing so many civilizations and cultures has obviously constituted a real problem; I have attempted to solve it by choosing that spelling I have judged most intelligible to the English-speaking world at the present date; but I should emphasize that ultimately these various choices have been mine, not those of the experts acknowledged above.

In particular I should like to thank the following: HM the Queen for gracious permission to quote from the Royal Archives at Windsor and Miss Jane Langton, late of the Royal Archives, for her assistance; Dr Chaim Herzog, President of Israel, for conversation on the subject of Golda Meir and permission to quote from material unpublished in this country; Dr Michael Grant for help and encouragement at many stages; Rana Kabbani for stimulating discussions and advice concerning the Arab world in general and Zenobia in particular, and General Moustapha Tlass, the Syrian Minister of Defence; my 'Georgian' consultants, the late Sir Charles Johnston (who first called Queen Tamara of Georgia to my attention), Mr Laurence Kelly, Professor Nico Kiasashvili of Tbilisi, and Mrs Katharine (Vivian) Ashton; and Dr Graham Webster and his wife Diana, not only for his help but for their hospitality. Mrs Maria Fairweather provided me with fascinating information concerning the reputation of Queen Jinga (Nzinga) in modern Angola; lastly the help of Angus Clarke and Daniel Johnson, who acted as my *occhi* and my *Augen* respectively, translating references to Matilda of Tuscany and Louise of Prussia, was invaluable.

I wish to thank the following for advice and/or support in many different ways: Dr R. J. Bingle of the India Office Library and Records; Dr Philip Crummy, Director of the Colchester Archaeological Trust; Mr Frank Delaney with whom I discussed the title at an early stage; Mr Donald Freed; Mr Tony Garratt who reminded me of Charles Doughty; Mr Tony Gregory of the Norfolk Archaeological Unit; Gale of the *Daily Telegraph* (Mr George Gale); Earl Gowrie; Mr Henry Grunwald, former Editor-in-Chief of Time Inc. for references to early Vietnamese heroines, and Ms Judy Stowe of BBC External Services for information concerning their reputation in modern Vietnam; Sir John Hale; Lady Selina Hastings; Mr Christopher Hibbert; Princess Antoinette Hohenlohe; Dr Lisa Jardine; Mr John Keegan; Lady Pansy Lamb; Professor Joyce Lebra-Chapman for illustrative material concerning the Rani of Jhansi; Professor Karl Leyser; Ms Sharon Macdonald; Miss Elizabeth Owles of the Moyses Hall Museum, Bury St Edmunds; Dame Felicity (Hanbury) Peake for recollections of her wartime service; Diana Phipps; Mr C. A. Price; Mr Denis Richards; the Hon. Hannah Rothschild; Mr David Spanier; Ms Dale Spender; Emma Tennant; Mr Michael Trend; Mr Paul Usherwood; Ms Kaari Utrio; Marina Warner; and Simone Warner who was my wonderful charioteer in the summer of 1985 when we explored East Anglia.

I have received editorial suggestions and advice from a galaxy of stars in the firmament of publishing, including Robert Gottlieb; Christopher Falkus, Juliet Gardiner and Linden Lawson, all of Weidenfeld's; Sunny Mehta of Knopf; and my agent Michael Shaw of Curtis Brown; Mr John Gillingham and Mr Alan Palmer provided helpful comments on the text; Ms Jane Blumberg checked the references and Mr Douglas Matthews of the London Library did the index: to each and all of these I have good reason to be profoundly grateful. As for Richard Bates, who created out of my unruly manuscript, with the aid of his word processor, the disks from which this book was set, it seems appropriate to quote the words of Henry James concerning art itself to express my thanks: 'I know of no substitute whatever for the force and beauty of its process'. Finally I must not forget the Home Team: from my son Orlando Fraser who did research for me at the Colindale Newspaper Library and elsewhere, and my daughter Flora Fraser Powell-Jones, always prepared to discuss the Classical world with energy, to my mother Elizabeth Longford, who may never have realized what an editorial burden lay ahead when she first encouraged me to read history. My husband Harold Pinter, although coming last in these acknowledgements, is always the first to read my work: no words of mine can express my debt to him sufficiently, so I will use his to thank him for his support when I ventured into 'quite remote ... utterly foreign ... territories'.

ANTONIA FRASER
St Cecilia's Day 1986
Feast of St Joseph 1988

Part One

CHAPTER ONE

A Singular Exception

~

> A singular exception . . . a woman is often acknow-
> ledged the absolute sovereign of a great kingdom, in
> which she would be deemed incapable of exercising the
> smallest employment, civil or military.
>
> GIBBON, Decline and Fall of the Roman Empire

Everyone knows about Boadicea. Every British school-
child learns her story: the stark tale of her stand against
the Romans 'flashes afresh to hold and horrify' with each
generation. Lest for a moment we forget her, on the banks of the
Thames, not far from the Houses of Parliament, she stands aloft
in her chariot, knives sprouting from its wheels; and it is in fact
those murderous knives which stamp our perception of her
indelibly. Hers is a gallant – and a savage story. Even as we bow
the knee, we shudder and step back as the Warrior Queen rides
by.

For all the strength of this image – depictions of Boadicea be
they in art or caricature are made instantly recognizable by use of
this detail – Boadicea's chariot did *not* actually have knives (or
scythes) affixed to its wheels. This is one of the very few
statements which can be made with any certainty concerning her.

Thus one of the most powerful figures in our history in terms
of popular imagination, one who did unquestionably exist in
that period assigned to her, unlike 'King' Arthur, no chivalric
monarch if he did exist but a sixth-century Romano British commander, survives by virtue of an image which is in itself spurious.
This is an apt illustration of the paradox which lies at the heart of
the subject of Queen Boadicea, and by extension that of the
Warrior Queen in general.

Of course the name Boadicea itself is not genuine either. That is the name generally employed in the prolific allusions made to her in contemporary society: it would be a rare day which did not produce at least one in the British Press.[1] This is something which is only partly dependent on the emergence of a female Prime Minister (although, as we shall see, certain specific military situations such as the Falklands War can produce a bristling harvest of such comparisons) since Boadicea's name can be and is invoked in a variety of different contexts. Nor is our own age unique in this respect, the unwithered 'infinite variety' of Queen Boadicea's images as perceived down our history being one of the themes of this book.

While Boadicea remains therefore the convenient name for what may be termed the fabulous Queen, driving her cruelly accoutred carriage (and it will be used for that Queen in this book), a clutch of other names have been proposed as being more plausible in relation to the woman herself. 'Our own honour, VOADICEA, or BOODICIA, by some BUNDUICA and BUNDUCA, Queene of the Iceni' was Ben Jonson's somewhat despairing description in *the Masque of Queenes*.[2] It is a desperation that a modern chronicler of Queen Boadicea's fortunes can share (although Ben Jonson cited only a few of the possible variants).

This uncertainty jostling the Warrior Queen's actual name, its spelling and derivation, may also be seen as part of the paradox: the extreme fame of Boadicea contrasts with the extreme ignorance and, in many instances, actual misapprehension about her. It is 'Boudicca', given by Tacitus, which is in fact the only contemporary rendering of the name which has come down to us. As a result it has been in the past 'relished by the learned' as Winston Churchill felicitously phrased it. 'Boadicea', sounding so different to our ears, is actually only two letters apart from Boudicca and the famous name is thus probably based on inaccurate transcriptions of Tacitus' Boudicca.[3]

In recent years however the learned have lost some of their relish for Boudicca. It is suggested, on philological evidence, that Tacitus too was in error: 'Boudica' must have been the correct

4

spelling. This brings the British Warrior Queen's name in line with the various Celtic words for victory, notably the Old Welsh *bouda*. It also means, happily, that Boadicea too can claim to be described as Queen Victoria (as was not infrequently noted in the late nineteenth century): for these two reasons, scholarly and sentimental, Boudica will be the name adopted for the historic figure who led the AD 60/61 rebellion against the Romans,[*] whereas Boadicea will be used for the legendary character.[4]

Others variants will be encountered and their origins traced in the course of Boadicea's latter-day history. At the moment it is enough to point out that this ambivalence towards Boadicea's name, like the misapprehensions concerning her career and circumstances, is also part of her aura: it has even allowed her at times to flourish under two separate identities.

In the late sixteenth century for example, an enterprising Florentine scholar-courtier named Petruccio Ubaldini, seeking royal patronage in England, wrote two volumes about the lives of illustrious ladies of yore and dedicated them to Queen Elizabeth. 'To satisfy the most pedantic readers', as he put it, he decided to divide the characters of Bonduica and Voadicia (although the distinction was of course a mistaken one arising out of the confusions produced by these endless variations of spelling). Faced with the stories of two queens which were, as he honestly admitted, astonishingly similar, Ubaldini boldly decided to derive a different moral from each. The moral of Bonduica's story is thus that 'Cruelty destroys any praise for honourable courage . . .'; that of Voadicia: 'Tyranny often brings intolerable wickedness which provokes in its victims a thirst for revenge . . .'[5]

As a matter of fact, both these morals can be derived quite correctly from Boadicea's story, although in modern parlance we

---

[*] The date of Boadicea's rebellion – AD 60 or 61 – is another matter in dispute. As to how Boudica is or was to be pronounced, one can only observe that an expedition of archaeological enquiry by the author to East Anglia in 1985 produced three separate pronunciations from the first three experts encountered: i.e. Bōūdica, Boudīca and Boudicā.

might prefer to transform Ubaldini's 'morals' into questions. Was Boadicea a savage attempting to destroy a superior civilization in a series of atrocities (and a *female* savage to boot . . .)? Or was she a patriotic leader rising up against an alien and brutal occupying power? Suffice it to say for the moment that in this respect the existence of so many variations of her name has evidently been a positive advantage in the promotion of her legend.

Thus the learneds' Boudica can easily possess quite different characteristics from the chariot-driving heroine aloft on London's Embankment without troubling the national consciousness too much. This celebrated Warrior Queen turns out to be like Proteus, he who could assume different shapes at will, beginning with her very name. Returning to Warrior Queens in general and the paradox which they present, it will be found that the protean quality is something which many of them have in common with Boadicea.

The central nature of this paradox can be stated as follows: whereas woman has on the whole, taking the rough with the smooth, the good epochs with the bad, been considered inferior to man throughout history, the arrival of a Warrior Queen, by whatever accident of fate, descent or sheer character, has been the signal for a remarkable outburst of excitement and even awe, sometimes accompanied by admiration and enthusiasm for her cause, beyond the ability of a mere male to arouse.

'In man's apparel . . . hanging about her the skins of beasts, before and behind, with a Sword about her neck, an Axe at her girdle, and a Bow and Arrows in her hand, leaping according to the custom, now here, now there, as nimbly as the most active among her attendants, all the while striking her Engema, that is, two Iron Bells, which serve her instead of Drums . . .'. Thus the Dutch Captain Fuller, commander of her personal bodyguard, admiringly described the seventeenth-century Queen Jinga of Angola, in her long battles against the Portuguese invaders. To Fuller, Jinga was 'A Cunning and Prudent Virago', despite or even because of her habit of keeping fifty or sixty young men as husbands (and another habit of human sacrifice); he served her faithfully for many years.[6]

6

Conversely, the emergence of a Warrior Queen has at other times been accompanied by disgust and fear at her very existence, emotions which would never be aroused by a male leader occupying the same position: Queen Jinga, the nightmare of the armed and voracious Amazon come to life, was viewed quite differently by her Portuguese enemies. To those on the other side, the actual atrocities committed or instigated by a woman leader bring about a special shudder, which recalls our reaction to the knives on Boadicea's chariot: it is not so much the mythical weapons themselves as the woman driving the chariot which gives us surely that special *frisson*.

Part of this *frisson* – of fear or admiration – is undoubtedly due to the fact that woman as a whole has been seen as a pacifying influence throughout history, this pacifying role being perceived as hers by nature and hers in duty. The whole question whether women actually *are* more pacific by nature is not the subject of the present book. For our purposes, it is however highly relevant that they have been perceived as such.

Some feminist writers have recently promulgated strongly the notion that a matriarchal society would or did lack the aggression that does and did characterize a patriarchal one. (Evidently non-pacific types such as Mrs Gandhi, Mrs Meir and Mrs Thatcher count as honorary men for the purposes of this argument because they have adopted masculine values in order to succeed in the patriarchal world.) 'And I know, in the depth of my being and in all my knowledge of history and humanity, I know women will struggle for a social order of peace, equality and joy' wrote the distinguished historian of women, Joan Kelly, in 1982, on the eve of her death. On the other hand, Lynne Segal, author of *Is the Future Female?*, expressed another view in an interview in 1987: 'I accept that women are gentler at the moment', but 'if they had the same amount of power as men, they wouldn't be more virtuous.'[7]

But the argument is not a novel one. The writings of Christine de Pisan in the fourteenth century drew attention to the pacifying potential of 'the good princess'. 'Supposed weakness is in fact often a moral strength,' she wrote, 'as when women, who are

7

physically weak and timid, are therefore more inclined to make peace and avert wars.' She added, citing the work of Queen Blanche, mother of St Louis: 'O God, how many great blessings in the world have often been caused by queens and princesses making peace between enemies.'[8] Thus in a sense the concept of the Warrior Queen cuts across not only man's view of woman's traditional weakness but also woman's view of her own ordained role as a peacemaker.

Nevertheless almost every culture throughout history has had its Warrior Queen or Queens either in fact or in fiction, or in some combination of them both. The United States of America is so far one of the significant exceptions in spite of 'the singular address and happy boldness' which Alexis de Tocqueville discovered in its unmarried young ladies as long ago as 1835. When a possible future Warrior Queen was presented in the 1984 Vice-Presidential Candidate Geraldine Ferraro, the reaction was, as will be seen, extremely uneasy. The Roman Empire, for all the host of noteworthy Empresses, those celebrated, strong-minded and sometimes disreputable women, was another *imperium* where an actual female reign would, as Gibbon pointed out, have appeared 'an inexpiable prodigy'.[9]

It is certainly of importance to the story of Boudica and her uprising against the Roman regime in Britain that she herself, in her gender as well as in her independence, bore something at least of the appearance of a prodigy, and an unwelcome one, to the occupying power. But of course both Rome then and the United States now have experience of dealings with foreign 'Warrior Queens'.

The opportunity should be taken to define the way in which the term will be understood in the present study. A potential Warrior Queen, in the modern sense, is one who might under certain circumstances have to take the decision to deploy her country's military resources. Thus for these purposes Mrs Thatcher at the time of the Falklands War played the Warrior Queen while Queen Elizabeth II was merely the reigning monarch. In the historical sense on the other hand, a Warrior

Queen will be regarded as one who combined both elements of rule and martial leadership. It must therefore be emphasized that Joan of Arc (although admittedly a frequent source of inspiration to many Warrior Queens) was not actually one herself in our terms. Since she led but did not rule, like the heroic 'General' Harriet Tubman, who commanded an action in the American Civil War, Joan of Arc belongs to that other wider category of Women Warriors, a fascinating but more diffuse subject than that of the present study: women having fought, literally fought, as a normal part of the army in far more epochs and far more civilizations than is generally appreciated.[10] Similarly Judith, the pious assassin of Holofernes (another frequently cited comparison) belongs to the category of Warrior Woman, or maid – although as a matter of fact the historical Judith was a widow.

If one examines a saying of Muhammad: 'The men perish if they obey the women', or another of his alleged quips regarding a princess on the Persian throne: 'No people who place a woman over their affairs prosper', the lesson of history does not exactly confirm the truth of this notion.[11] On the contrary a Warrior Queen – or female ruler – has often provided the focus for what a country afterwards perceived to have been its golden age; beyond the obvious example (to the English) of Queen Elizabeth I, one might cite the twelfth-century Queen Tamara of Georgia, or the fifteenth-century Isabella of Spain. The extra value of a Warrior Queen as a rallying point for the chivalric feelings of her nation will be one of the recurring themes of this book.

Returning to America and its present culture, the United States does of course lack a hereditary monarchy, which for better or for worse is a system inclined to throw up such things as queens, and thus by implication Warrior Queens, from time to time. The irony of this situation was summed up by Gibbon:

> In every and age and country, the wiser, or at least the stronger, of the two sexes has usurped the powers of the State, and confined the other to the cares and pleasures of domestic life. In hereditary monarchies, however, and

especially in those of modern Europe, the gallant spirit of chivalry, and the law of succession, have accustomed us to allow a singular exception; and a woman is often acknowledged the absolute sovereign of a great kingdom, in which she would be deemed incapable of exercising the smallest employment, civil or military.[12]

So we have an extension to the paradox of the Warrior Queen: the phenomenon is found almost everywhere (if not within a culture, by conflict with another culture); yet the person concerned is generally regarded as the 'singular exception' and that very singularity for better or for worse provides her aura.

There is after all a good deal to be said – in purely practical terms – for General de Gaulle's view of the omnipresence of force in history: 'Is it possible to conceive of life without force?' He wrote in *The Edge of the Sword*: 'Force has watched over civilization in the cradle: force has ruled empires, and dug the grave of decadence . . . It is true to say that the fighting spirit, the art of war, the virtues of the soldier are an integral part of man's inheritance. They have been part and parcel of history in all its phases, the medium through which it has expressed itself.' He concluded that 'the noblest teachings of philosophy and religion have found no higher ideals' than those of 'self-sacrifice for the sake of the community, suffering made glorious – these two things which are the basic elements of the profession of arms'.[13]

One can gainsay de Gaulle's conclusion, or at least his overall description of the profession of arms, without contradicting his general – and even obvious – point that history can be interpreted at one level as the history of 'force'. If this be true, and, more importantly, society itself has believed it to be true, then on the one hand the traditional lack of involvement of woman in the world of 'force' will add to her air of inferiority; on the other hand her involvement in that world, when it occurs, stands a good chance of raising her status. As Tacitus wrote of the warlike Germans: 'Renown is easiest won among perils.'[14] To put it another way, many women leaders have found in the crucible of war – if successfully survived – the fiery process which has guaranteed them passage into the realms of honorary men.

It is because 'all history has been made by men' and 'it is still a world that belongs to men', in the words of Simone de Beauvoir, that the characters and careers of those women who have been the singular exceptions become crucial.[15] Such careers have always afforded much of interest to both sexes, not just because a tradition of independent womanhood is kept alive for the female sex in darker days. The same names will be found recited over and over again like an encouraging (or admonitory) litany the moment a new Warrior Queen appears. Not merely Boadicea herself, but Penthesilea, Judith, Semiramis and Zenobia from ancient times are invoked in this roll-call of the armed and female faithful. Zenobia drew upon comparisons to Cleopatra, from whom she claimed to be descended. Dio Cassius compared Boadicea to Semiramis. Elizabeth I and Catherine the Great, frequently compared in their own time to the above (Catherine to her admiring correspondent Voltaire was his 'Semiramis of the North'), themselves provided the rich sources of historical comparison.[16]

An appeal to bygone 'heroines' as a source of strength and above all validity would indeed appear to be exceptionally important where female leaders are concerned, down to our own day. The unnatural, even bizarre aspect of a woman in such a role – 'that boisterousness with which she terrifies us', in the words of an eighteenth-century commentator on Boadicea – is thus tacitly admitted, before being justified by this sonorous appeal to the past. The names of the 'heroines' cited do of course vary to a certain degree – but not nearly as much as the character and circumstances of the women citing them. At the time of the Falklands War, Mrs Thatcher as Prime Minister neatly recalled Queen Victoria by quoting her in a television broadcast: 'Failure? The possibilities do not exist.'[17] The evocation of the strong and successful female image was surely as important as the sentiment, although inspection reveals little in common between the nine-teenth-century hereditary monarch and the late-twentieth-century democratically elected leader – except their sex.

It is also true that exactly the same names from this important but limited female pantheon can be used to insult, while the nature of the insult can also vary. When Denis Healey, as a senior Labour statesman, reflected that Mrs Thatcher reminded him 'very much' of Catherine the Great, he was not of course referring to the former's impeccable private life, but to the imperiousness 'allied to a temperament which is in many ways very masculine' which he considered both ladies had in common.[18] Yet the allusion to Catherine the Great, Voltaire's 'Semiramis of the North', like that to Semiramis herself, is one which could in different circumstances bear a sexual connotation, since both the ninth-century BC Semiramis and the eighteenth-century AD Catherine the Great might be described, at least in popular terms, as 'a great sovereign and a great lover'. Boccaccio in the fourteenth century delineated Semiramis as one who on the one hand showed 'that in order to govern it is not necessary to be a man, but to have courage', and on the other hand 'gave herself to many men' along the way.[19]

The presumed sexual voracity of a Warrior Queen, at least up till the twentieth century, will be found to be one of the recurring themes of her treatment at the hands of her contemporaries and of history. Conversely, but not contradictorily, another theme will be found to be her chastity: on occasion maintained, according to the myth, under the most remarkable circumstances – against all the available evidence. Sometimes the same woman – such as Matilda of Tuscany, whom we shall find leading her men in the cause of the eleventh-century Pope Gregory VII – bears both accusations. This treatment of the Warrior Queen as a supernaturally chaste creature, put against that other image of her as preternaturally lustful (the Voracity Syndrome), seems to indicate that, because her sex is first and foremost what makes the Warrior Queen remarkable, her sexuality must always be called into question as well.

Other themes will be found to occur and recur: that of the Holy (and sometimes Armed) Figurehead is one of them, from the Arab Lady of Victory to Isabella the Catholic, scourge of the Spanish Moors (such characters frequently also forming part of the Chaste Syndrome). Then the Appendage Syndrome runs through the whole book: the stressed connection of so many Warrior Queens to the nearest strong masculine figure. In turn the Shame Syndrome, whereby all the surrounding masculine figures are described as failing in courage compared to the Warrior Queen herself, underlines in another way the purely masculine context in which most Warrior Queens have operated. It is this context which has enabled many a Warrior Queen, endowed with a partner, to be hailed as the 'Better-Man' (of the two). Conversely, the 'Only-a-Weak-Woman' Syndrome has the normally robust female leader indulging in a sudden diplomatic outbreak of modesty, pleading the notorious weakness of her sex, generally for good practical reasons of self-interest.

It is indeed this recurrence of themes which gives the Warrior Queens chosen for discussion here their special significance. As has been stated, this is not intended to be an encyclopaedic work on a vast subject, and even such compelling figures as the real, not the operatic, Brünnhilde, a sixth-century Visigothic Queen of Austrasia, or the ferocious Nanny, wife of Old Cudjoe, chief of the Maroons, who led a seventeenth-century uprising in Jamaica, do not necessarily find a place in it.[20]

One important theme may be termed the Tomboy Syndrome, whereby the Warrior Queen in youth, all unknowing of her martial destiny, is depicted as unconsciously eschewing dolls in favour of soldiers, domestic pursuits in favour of hunting.[21] The Tomboy Syndrome in particular demonstrates the perpetual need for reassurance which the emergence of a Warrior Queen seems to evoke: this woman is not like other women, runs the refrain; this being so, her strangeness should be established from the start. A quotation from the start of one of the many historical romances in English on the subject of Boadicea shows that the British Queen is certainly not immune from the syndrome: 'Wait for us, Boadicea! That horse of yours must have invisible wings to carry you at such speed.' So runs *Boadicea* by Betty King, published in 1975.[22] (Absolutely nothing is in fact known about the childhood of Boadicea.)

Boadicea is selected as the pivot of this book partly for the fascinating combination of fame and ambiguity which her career provides, partly because so many of the themes which recur in the treatment of other Warrior Queens are raised in her story and its subsequent treatment. Stories of these other historic Warrior Queens are brought forward where relevant not only to supplement hers but also to illustrate the universality of the subject. But it is Boadicea who is a convenient starting-point, and Boadicea who is the engrossing exemplar.

Nevertheless the first task, before turning to the true story of Boudica in her own time, in so far as it can be established, must be to look back into the depths of time and culture. Is there something primitive in the human heart which can be held accountable for the mingled awe, horror, and ecstasy which so often attends the manifestation of a Warrior Queen in our midst? Is it the deep-rooted allegiance which we owe to the idea of woman-as-goddess which makes her fleshy apparition before us, fully armed, in the guise of the Warrior Queen so thrillingly traumatic?

Let us begin with the Celtic goddess and see how far chariot-driving Boadicea descends from her: for it is to her, if anyone, that Boudica must have been related in the perception of her British contemporaries, those who teemed after her.

CHAPTER TWO

Antique Glories

Where is the antique glory now become
That whilom wont in women to appear?

SPENSER, The Faerie Queene

Goddesses stalk the land in the Celtic mythology, ride their chargers, drive their chariots, fight their battles, are vanquished – sometimes – and more often than not emerge victorious. Nor was the sexuality of these deities ignored, as was appropriate in goddesses who were connected with birth (and the fertility of the earth and crops) as well as with war and its companion death. The concept of the Celtic Great Mother, overlording the other lesser tribal deities, may or may not have been universally known (although it was certainly known); what is evident is the rampant and rich nature of the female deities who paraded through the Celtic world. The precise relationship of goddess to goddess may also be impossible to determine – these were after all deities of a non-literate society, whose tales were finally written down hundreds of years after they had first been sung, chanted and spoken to Celtic audiences. What is evident is that a series of female 'High Ones' were celebrated in the epics.[1]

Furthermore, in the Celtic world, again and again it is the magic intervention in the course of battle of a female, goddess, queen or a combination of the two, which provides the focus or climax of the story. Such a female may be a hag or a beauty (or one disguised as the other). She may be as Rhiannon, the horse goddess of the Welsh *Mabinogion,* 'a woman dressed in shining gold brocade and riding a great pale horse' or in the nine sorceresses of Gloucester encountered in the same sequence of tales who laid waste the country in their helmets and headpieces before the champion Peredur finally smote them. [2]

The name of the Welsh Rhiannon connects to the Celtic Rigantona, great queen or 'Queen of the Demons'; she in turn links to the Morrigan, sometimes merely a sinister (and sexually active) raven-goddess of war and sometimes used as a composite name to denote a trio, Badbh, Nemain and Macha, all with strong connections to both fertility and battle.[3] Above all there is the character of Queen Medb (or Maeve) who is to the great Celtic cycle of *The Tain* what the Greek goddesses are to *The Iliad*, the physique and appetites of a woman, the magic powers of a goddess.

It can indeed be argued that Queen Medb is the true heroine of *The Tain*; for although the champion Cúchulainn, the Hound of Ulster, is unarguably its hero, Medb, his adversary, is the female protagonist, a vivid character in her own right, both glamorous and ferocious, and it is her ardent desire to secure the Brown Bull of Ulster which sets the whole cycle in train. Like the *Mabinogion*, *The Tain* first emerges in written form long after its stories must first have been current, in the case of *The Tain* Christianized by monks in the eighth century AD (as it was later to be bowdlerized by Lady Gregory). But the society which *The Tain* actually reflects is thought to be placed around the time of the birth of Christ – that is to say some sixty years before the Boudican revolt.[4]

At the start of *The Tain*, Medb is having 'pillow talk' with her husband Ailill, her theme being her superior state before she got married – not an unusual theme for such conversations, perhaps, but Medb is able to back her claim by pointing out that she was the daughter of the High King of Ireland, the 'last and haughtiest' of his six daughters: 'I outdid them in grace and giving and battle and warlike combat', she boasts; moreover she controlled fifteen hundred soldiers and as many freeborn native men.

Ailill responds that he too is a king, by descent from his mother (a queen). It is however as they wrangle on the subject of possessions, the pair matching bull for bull, that Medb has to admit that one of Ailill's bulls is finer than all of hers, since her own star animal, Finnbennach, has deserted to the King's herd, after refusing to be led by a woman. Since the finest bull in all Ulster is known to be the Donn Cuailnge – the Brown Bull of Ulster – Medb determines to secure him with her Connaughtian army, and vanquish her husband's claims. In this fashion begins the long epic of *The Tain*, glorious and bloodstained, the most magnificent cattle raid in literature, with Medb leading the attack and Cúchulainn as the champion of Ulster attempting to defend the Brown Bull from her rapacity.

Where Medb's character is concerned, she is certainly both cunning and imperious as well as lustful (her behaviour in that respect certainly forms part of the Voracity Syndrome). It is also noticeable that when she does suggest breaking the rules of fair fight, this deviousness is ascribed to her sex. On one occasion Medb suggests, from the vantage point of her chariot, that certain people, currently friendly but potentially hostile, be killed as a safeguard. Ailill condemns this as 'a woman's thinking' – and wicked. When Medb sleeps with the warrior Fergus in order to seduce him to her side, Ailill forgives Fergus with the consoling words: 'I know all about queens and women, I lay first fault straight at women's own sweet swellings and loving lust'.

Cúchulainn is the persistent target of the Queen's attempted treachery. Medb first suggests a truce and then secretly sends six soldiers against the champion, all of royal blood (fortunately Cúchulainn is able to slay all six). Medb then suggests a private meeting between Cúchulainn and herself, promising to be attended only by her unarmed women. Cúchulainn's own charioteer warns him against such a dangerous rendezvous: 'Medb is a forceful woman. I'd watch out for her hand at my back.' So Cúchulainn does at least take along his sword – which is just as well, because he finds the rendezvous has actually turned into an encounter with fourteen armed warriors. (Fortunately Cúchulainn is able once again to despatch the whole lot.)

Queen Medb, with the magical birds or squirrels on her shoulders, is not the only strong goddess–woman in the Celtic legends. Part of Cúchulainn's training as a fighter consists of his encounter with Aife, 'the hardest woman warrior in the world', while Cúchulainn himself is being trained in arms by another woman named Scathach. But it is the physical description of Queen Medb which seems to sum up the type of the Celtic goddess-cum-warrior. This is the fighting Queen Medb, as described to Cúchulainn by his fellow warrior Cethern, grievously wounded by an unknown assailant. 'A tall, fair, long-faced woman with soft features came at me . . . She had a head of yellow hair and two gold birds on her shoulders. She wore a purple cloak folded about her, with five hands' breadth of gold on her back. She carried a light, stinging, sharp-edged lance in her hand, and she held an iron sword with a woman's grip over her head – a massive figure. It was she who came against me first.'

'Then I'm sorry for you,' is Cúchulainn's comment. 'That was Medb of Cruachan.'

The connection between the insubstantial if vigorous goddess and the historic figure of the Warrior Queen remains for all this an elusive if fascinating one. If we take a character like Semiramis, the ninth-century BC Queen of Babylon who did exist but whose legend far outstrips her historical reality, it is clear that her identification with the goddess Astarte formed a valuable part of that legend in the mind of posterity. Eight centuries later we find the Hellenistic Queen Cleopatra deliberately donning the mantle of the goddess Isis for sound political reasons. The reporting of Boudica by Dio Cassius, which will be discussed later, suggests that she was herself conforming to some kind of stereotype of the Celtic warrior–woman; this in turn derived from the infinitely powerful character of the Celtic mother-cum-war-goddess, like Medb.

Such attempts on the part of the ancient Warrior Queens to assume the mystical authority of the War Goddess were obviously linked with the prevalence of these martial goddess figures. Let us suppose that together they constitute proof that there is something deep in the human spirit which finds in the image of the strong and armed woman a figure of awe. If that be so, then the next step is to consider whether such awe springs not so much from the human subconscious as from some real state of society in the remote past. Is it possible that the aggressive goddess, far from being a surprising figure, in terms of the patriarchal attitudes which have generally prevailed, is actually a reflection of the preceding *matriarchal* age when women as a whole were the dominant sex? Thus the Warrior Queen herself might appear as a kind of vestigial relic of that distant epoch: hence her encouraging or terrifying aspect according to the contemporary view taken of women's rightful role in society.

It is certainly tempting to regard the chariot-driving Warrior Queen as owing her authority to deep memories of a matriarchal society where women either held the reins of the chariot or gave the men the orders which enabled them to do so. Matriarchy has always been an attractive concept (to some). On the one hand a nostalgic conviction that there was a golden age when women enjoyed a now vanished prestige is comforting to the oppressed. This is the age whose passing Spenser mourned in *The Faerie Queene*:

> Where is the antique glory now become
> That whilom wont in women to appear? [5]

On the other hand, more vigorously, a remedy for the future is suggested by this nostalgia, to restore what was evidently Nature's intended ordering.

Interest in the notion of matriarchy, keen in our own day as an obvious development of the rise of feminism, is nevertheless not exclusive to it. In particular, the influential work of J. S. Bachofen, first published in 1861, supposed the existence of 'mother right', a pre-Classical and pre-Biblical culture of the Bronze Age. Ending around 1200 BC, this was a culture in which the male role in procreation was ignored, and descent was traced only in the female line. Bachofen found examples of such matriarchal societies in places as diverse as Lycia, Athens, Crete, Lemnos, Egypt, Tibet, Central Asia and India. [6]

More recently, however, scholars have been stepping warily where such positive statements concerning historical matriarchies are concerned. It is suggested that the archaeological discoveries of women buried with horses and spears – for example the Sarmatian graves of the fourth century BC – may point to the presence of women in the fighting force, but that in itself does not necessarily suppose a matriarchy.* [7] After all, if the graves of females who have served in the Israeli army were to be discovered in a thousand years' time, it would be a mistake on the part of scholars to regard this as proof of a matriarchal organization in the Israeli state. In 1986 shortage of recruits in the prolonged Iraq–Iran war led to girls being sent into battle, pictured in the newspapers dressed in the chador and carrying a gun: their skeletons, surviving by chance alongside their guns, would give an even more distorted picture of the Muslim state if some kind of 'matriarchal' conclusion were drawn.

Replacing the belief in actual matriarchies, it is now supposed that while certain strong-minded Bronze Age queens did exist, just as individual women in certain societies of the past did display at least something of Spenser's 'antique glory', the status of women as a whole was not superior to that of men. The existence of these spirited and respected individuals represents a state of affairs which is a far cry from the dreams of true matriarchy and matrilineal succession, the evidence for which has been described, even in the free Celtic world from which Boudica sprang, as being 'very dubious' and 'best consigned to the large corpus of myths surrounding Celtic society'. [8] It seems, as with the clearly legendary goddesses of war, that it is the continued tradition of pre-Classical matriarchies which is important here, rather than the fact of their existence.

The question of historical truth becomes even more acute in

---

* The *Oxford English Dictionary* (1933) definition of 'matriarchy' is: 'That form of social organization where the mother, not the father, is the head of the family, and in which descent and relationships are reckoned through mothers not fathers.' The *Concise Oxford Dictionary of Current English Usage* (1963), in its entry for the word 'matriarch', adds: 'usually jocular'.

the case of the Amazons and their leaders, including most prominently Penthesilea and Hippolyta. Like the alleged early pre-Classical matriarchies, the Amazons have sometimes been granted a proper historical existence; however in their case the evidence actually comes from the Classical writers, most notably Herodotus.[9] If true, this would be another interesting possibility to explore with regard to the nature of the Warrior Queen's origins: should we look to these colonies of armed and self-mutilated women for inspiration? (They were supposed to remove one breast for the sake of drawing the bow: the name Amazon itself was once thought to derive from the Greek 'without breast'.) Many of the ancient writers site the Amazons in an area around the Black Sea, and indeed if they are allowed a historical existence, what is now Northern Anatolia seems the likeliest place for the cradle; coincidentally or not, the lands contiguous to the Black Sea will also provide a number of indisputably authentic Warrior Queens. Scythia to the north however also has its claims. Herodotus, on the other hand, supported by Diodorus Siculus, places his armed maidens on the shores of the Mediterranean in Libya, the significant point being that the Classical writers in general situated the Amazons on the outskirts of their known world, and as this world expanded, so the kingdoms of the Amazons receded into more distant territories.

Outside the known world of the Greeks lay the barbarians – those rude and unfortunate strangers who lacked the brilliant order of the Greek state, and it is to this realm of disorderliness and unnaturalness that the Greek tradition of the Amazons belonged.[10] Thus the Greek heroes of legend are frequently found undergoing a kind of ritual encounter with an Amazon, from which the Greek emerges the victor – the point being less the victory of one sex over the other (since the superiority of the male sex would be taken for granted by the Greeks) than the subjugation of the barbarians by the forces of civilization: it was one of the labours of Hercules to secure the girdle of the Amazon Queen Hippolyta. Similarly in art, Amazonomachy was a popular theme for many temple friezes and vases: but the defeated women there depicted actually stood for the Greek's victories over their male enemies – such as the Persians.

Diodorus Siculus, writing in about 40 BC, has, like Homer, Penthesilea involving her Amazons in the Trojan War, in support of Priam, and being killed as a result by Achilles: after that the power and prestige of the Amazons declined. And it was the defeat and death of the 'Amazonian' Camilla of the Volscians, described by Virgil in *The Aeneid*, which presaged the establishment of the new Roman Empire under Aeneas.[11]

Camilla is introduced to us at the head of 'her cavalcade of squadrons a-flower with bronze'. She is among the Italian leaders who have gathered together, hoping to expel the invading Trojans led by Aeneas from their native land: a maiden warrior so fleet of foot that she could run across a field of corn without damaging the blades, across the sea without wetting the soles of her feet. Her description also provides an excellent Classical example of the Tomboy Syndrome: 'She was a warrior; her girl's hands had never been trained to Minerva's distaff and her baskets of wool, but rather, though a maid, she was one to face out grim fights and in speed of foot to out-distance the winds . . .' As Camilla passed, wayfarers gaped 'to see how regal splendour clothed her smooth shoulders in purple, how her brooch clasped her hair in its gold, and how she wore on her a Lycian quiver and carried a shepherd's myrtle staff with a lance's head'.

In the final military confrontation with Aeneas Camilla rides 'armed with her quiver, exulting like an Amazon, through the midst of the slaughter, having one breast exposed for freedom in the fight. Sometimes with all her strength she would be casting her tough spear-shafts in dense showers, and sometimes without pause for rest her hand would wield a stout battle-axe.' Camilla is surrounded by her faithful female attendants ('daughters of Italy') equally bold in the affray, Larina, Tulla and Tarpeia 'wielding her bronze axe'; Virgil compares them directly to the Amazons of Thrace, 'who, warring in their brilliant accoutrements, make Thermodon's streams echo to the hoof-beats, as they ride, it

22

may be with Hippolyta, or else when martial Penthesilea drives back in her chariot from war, and her soldier-women, shrieking wild battle-cries, exult as they wave their crescent shields'.

Camilla's previous exploits – man-killing on a vicious scale – are related in gory detail ('She battered through his unguarded breast with her long firwood-shafted spear', etc. etc.), as is Camilla's pride in her achievements. Here she addresses the mighty hunter Ornytus, whom she has pierced through: 'Etruscan, did you imagine that you were chasing wild beasts in a forest? Well, the day will come which will prove that you and your fellows imagined wrongly; and it will be proved through a woman's weapons. Yet you shall carry to the spirits of your fathers no mean fame – the fame of falling by Camilla's spear.'

In the end Camilla does fall to a man: it is the javelin of Arruns, whistling out of the blue which smites her down, signalling the defeat of the Italian cause. But Arruns only succeeds with the direct intervention of Phoebus Apollo; and subsequently Diana, the goddess Camilla serves, sees to it that her sentinel Opis avenges the Volscian's death: 'Your passing shall not be without fame throughout the world.'

It is indeed the fame of the Amazons, and prototypes such as Camilla, which foreshadows the Warrior Queen, rather than the historical truth of their existence. Again and again we shall find a Warrior Queen acting out her life voluntarily or involuntarily as an example of the Appendage Syndrome: that is to say, she will either be regarded officially as an appendage to her father, husband or even son (as in the case of Cleopatra) or stress the relationship to give herself validity (as in Elizabeth I's frequent stress upon her father Henry VIII). The Amazons of legend, however, specifically derived their exotic quality from the fact that they were nobody's appendage.

The latter-day reputation of the Amazons and their imitators was expressed by Thomas Heywood in his popular *Gynaekeion or Nine Bookes of Various History Concerning Women*, first printed in 1624. He praised Camilla for being the product of a tomboy upbringing by her father: for taking a vow of chastity to concentrate on the hunting and killing of wild beasts. Heywood translated Virgil's account of Camilla in battle array with verve if not melody:

> To their supply Camilla came
> The gallant Volscian lass
> Who bravely did command the horse
> With troops that shin'd in brass.[12]

The fact that the Classical writers described the Amazons originally as an example of how badly things would turn out if the world was turned upside down and women ruled was disregarded. Ironically, John Knox, approvingly citing Aristotle on the 'monstrousness' of the Amazons, as he thundered against female rule in the mid-sixteenth century ('their strength weakness, the counsel foolishness and judgment frenzy') was in fact on firm historical ground.[13] It could even be argued that the perversity with which the French King Henri III had male *mignons* dress up as (female) Amazons at the court of the 1570s had something to be said for it historically: for it reflected the original concept of the Amazon kingdom as a place in which the natural order had been turned upside down.

The Warrior Queens cheerfully ignored all this. In any situation in which a female ruler had perforce to involve herself in war, an allusion to the Amazons was an appeal to history for the verification of her role. Queen Louise of Prussia, the exquisite fragile butterfly whom Napoleon would break on the wheel despite her valiant spirit, was contemptuously described by him as appearing on the battlefield 'dressed as an Amazon in the uniform of her regiment of dragoons'.[14] Napoleon did not want pretty women on the battlefield dressed as Amazons or anything else; but to the Prussian soldiers who cheered the straightforward patriotism of their lovely queen (in contrast to the vacillation of her husband) the deliberate assumption of male uniform by a highly feminine woman was an inspiring symbol.

Eleanor of Aquitaine was the great feudal heiress whose

marriage to Louis VII of France in 1137, shortly after the death of her father, brought him vast possessions. At the time of her marriage Eleanor was only fifteen and the complicated future which awaited her, gifted as she was with beauty, riches and the intelligence to make use of her gifts, could hardly have been foreseen: the marriage itself would end in divorce, following which the heiress Eleanor would wed the rival monarch across the water, Henry II of England. Eleanor therefore was still a comparatively young woman on that Easter Day 1146 when she knelt before the celebrated orator, the Abbé Bernard of Clairvaux at Vézelay, and, moved by his eloquence, offered him her thousands of vassals for what was to become the Second Crusade.[15] She was attended by numerous 'ladies of quality' as she knelt, bearers of such heraldic names as Sybille Countess of Flanders, Mamille of Roucy, Florine of Bourgogne, Torqueri of Bouillon and Faydide of Toulouse.

It was one thing for a great lady to pledge her vassals, quite another for her to go on the crusade herself. This however was what Queen Eleanor proceeded to do, and opinions have varied concerning the reason. Did chivalry demand the presence of a woman at the centre of this pious procession? More humanly, did King Louis himself fear for the consequences of leaving his fascinating young wife at home? Whatever the reason, the chronicler who related the episode considered that the Queen's departure, surrounded by her ladies, set an extremely bad example to the female sex as a whole. Furthermore the papal bull which promulgated the Crusade, and which was read aloud at Vézelay, expressly forbade the attendance of concubines on the expedition.

It was at this point, according to legend, that Queen Eleanor suddenly appeared among the crowds at Vézelay 'taking the cross', riding a white horse and herself dressed in the guise of an Amazon, with gilded buskins on her feet and plumes in her hair. Surrounded by her ladies, similarly if less gorgeously attired, the Queen galloped through crowds, urging on the faithful to join the Crusade in a deliberate imitation of Penthesilea and her 'soldier–women'. Her squadron of ladies also distributed white distaffs to the fainthearted – an early form of the First World War's white feather.

According to Nicetas, the Queen kept up her enjoyable Classical charade along the route to the Holy Land. The Greek historian wrote of the 'women dressed as men, mounted on horses and armed with lance and battle axe' that they 'kept a martial mien, bold as Amazons'. And he mentioned that at the head, 'one in particular [presumably Eleanor] richly dressed . . . went by the name of the "lady of the golden boot", the elegance of her bearing and the freedom of her movements recalling the celebrated leader of the Amazons'.[16]

In a bold gesture, Queen Eleanor had thus separated herself from the category of mortal women, mere concubines (albeit royal) and other female companions; by her plumes and her bold buskins she had appealed ostentatiously to the past, and declared in so doing her right to accompany the Crusade. It should perhaps be noted in conclusion that the bull for the next Crusade – the Third Crusade of 1189 – expressly forbade women of all sorts to join the expedition by general agreement of all the Christian monarchs including King Louis. But by this time Queen Eleanor had been married to King Henry II of England for nearly forty years.

The problem which faced Eleanor's descendant, Anne, Queen of England from 1702 and of Great Britain from 1707, was one not so much of action as of image. Unlike her sister Mary, in the preceding reign, Queen Anne had no William III at her side as consort, co-ruler and in effect sole controller of the destinies of the country. It was clear that William after Queen Mary's death in 1694 was as much a *de facto* ruler by right of his male sex as a *de jure* monarch. Queen Anne on the other hand had as her consort the dim Danish Prince George who had no claims to the English throne, and whom no one considered making *de facto* ruler. Yet Anne reigned throughout a period of extraordinary military activity in the history of her country, ending gloriously with the victorious Marlborough campaigns, but coming perilously close to defeat before that happy outcome was achieved.

Across the Channel, Anne's cousin, Louis xiv, the Sun King, had long dazzled his compatriots with his martial exploits. How was Queen Anne, a middle-aged lady in poor health at the time of her accession, to present an image which was both imposing and opposing? As a younger woman she had had recourse to the traditional training of many Warrior Queens and loved to ride, as though to emulate some legendary goddess of the chase. Swift described Queen Anne out hunting, attired in dark cloak and hood, driving her one-horsed chaise 'furiously like Jehu, and as a mighty hunter like Nimrod' (a Boadicean as well as a biblical image). Later the Queen's enormous weight, following seventeen ill-fated pregnancies, caused her to take a 'chariot' with huge wheels.[17]

The age of the active warrior monarch was drawing to a close (George ii, in the next reign but one, was the last British monarch to lead his own army in battle) but was not yet concluded. Since Queen Anne, for all her command, both titular and actual, of the army and navy, could scarcely fulfil the practical obligations of a commander-in-chief, art and fantasy had to be called into play. Verrio painted the Queen as Justice for the ceiling of Hampton Court Palace, armed with a sword and holding a pair of scales. At a state visit to Bath, for example, Queen Anne was surrounded by a guard of honour of virgins 'richly attired like Amazons with bows and arrows', and others who danced beside her coach. Verses solemnizing the Vigo Bay thanksgiving at St Paul's in 1702 thundered a sonorous message:

> As threat-ning Spain did to Eliza bow
> So France and Spain shall do to Anna now . . .

The reality was very different as Sir John Clerk, one of the Scots commissioners, wrote in his memoirs: a gouty old woman with a red spotted face, some nasty bandages and a poultice.[18]

Nor has the allusion to the Amazons been deemed to lose its usefulness in the modern age: in 1986, for example, the women surrounding Benazir Bhutto, bold female claimant to the leadership of Pakistan, are colloquially known as 'The Amazons'.[19] Yet no appeal to the (incorrectly interpreted) past for validation seems more touching and more paradoxical than that made on the magnificent tombstone of Matilda of Tuscany, constructed on a significantly heroic scale following her death in 1115.

It was held to be appropriate that some allusion to her career on the battlefield should be made, apart from the four huge female figures of Prudence, Justice, Fortitude and Temperance which supported the tomb. So Penthesilea was called into play: *Et tunc disposuit turmes invicta Virago Qualis Amazonide Penthesilea solet* (And then this warrior-woman disposed her troops as the Amazonian Penthesilea is accustomed to do).[20] Thus the deeply religious Christian Countess Matilda, whose personal crusade was on behalf of the Pope, for the empire of Christ, needed the imprimatur of the savage pagan Queen to justify her unwomanly role.

CHAPTER THREE

The Queen of War

~

I am the queen of war. I am the queen of the thunderbolt.
I stir up the sea and calm it. I am the rays of the Sun.

PTOLEMAIC CREED OF THE GODDESS ISIS

Flesh-and-blood Warrior Queens – stepping out from behind the image of the war goddess – were not unknown to the ancient world; in general their activities were zestfully chronicled, particularly if some lesson could be derived to the detriment of the contemporary male, whether as leader or soldier. For there is a new element introduced by the reality of reported history – or what passes for such – and one which will emerge significantly with many a Warrior Queen including Boudica herself when she proposed the alternative of victory or death: 'This is what I, as a woman, plan to do: – let the men live in slavery if they will.'[1]

This is what might be termed the Shame Syndrome: not only is it wondrous to find a mere woman acting in a martial manner, but in so doing the woman concerned shows up, positively *shames* the weaker males who surround her. The earlier goddess–women were in a sense not able to shame the males they encountered since their supernatural powers clearly placed them in a superior position from the start.

On the other hand the titivating theme of sexual licence, the Voracity Syndrome, is, if anything, developed with the emergence of the flesh-and-blood woman. Lust (especially on the part of a widow, the status of so many Warrior Queens, presumably denied that to which she had become agreeably accustomed) remained a popular vice to associate with the name of a female leader, just as it had been a characteristic of a Celtic goddess.

Of course the trailing clouds of the goddess linger. In the case of Semiramis, zest caused the Greek writers to outrun the historical facts and gleefully transform an Assyrian ruler of the ninth century BC into a demi-legendary creature. The historical basis for Semiramis is one Sammu-ramat, the Babylonian widow of the Assyrian King Shamshi-Adad V, and mother of his heir Adad-nirari III. On Shamshi-Adad's death in 811 BC, Queen Sammu-ramat ruled as regent for five years during the minority of her son; beyond the fact that her regency was energetic, which suggests a strong character, little else is known for certain concerning her.[2]

In the hands of the Greeks, Semiramis became a daring character, subject to a series of adventures from birth; being the daughter of the goddess Derceto by an Assyrian, she was exposed in the desert, only to have her life saved by doves, who succoured her for a year. Subsequently she was brought up by a peasant until her beauty secured her two profitable marriages – first to the Governor of Ninevah, and then to Ninus King of Assyria.

Herodotus made Semiramis responsible for some of the remarkable embellishments to the city of Ninevah, which moderated the flooding of the river (although he rated her intelligence lower than that of a succeeding queen, Ninocris); while Propertius wrote that 'with dams Euphrates she controlled, where through her capital it rolled'.[3] But Semiramis' plans for rebuilding Ninevah were less important to her legend than the use she was alleged to have made of her beauty, securing the throne itself from her doting husband Ninus. Having been proclaimed sole Empress of Assyria, Semiramis lost no time in having the foolish Ninus put to death. Unencumbered by male tutelage, she further glorified her capital Babylon, in the time she spared from her military campaigns, by means of which she conquered many of the neighbouring countries of Mesopotamia.

Semiramis, pattern of the Warrior Queen who was nevertheless all woman, was said on one occasion to have been at her toilette when the news was brought to her that Babylon had revolted. Half-dressed, she swore to quell the insurrection before her toilette should be completed. Her voracious sexual appetites were, like the Queen herself, legendary; the most stalwart soldiers under her command were regularly called into a different kind of service; ungratefully if practically, Semiramis was in the habit of putting her lovers to death immediately after a night of love lest the tale of the Empress's desires should be spread abroad. Even more licentious, as well as unnatural, was the passion that Semiramis was supposed to have nourished for her son Ninyas (which in one version of her story caused him to kill her).

At least on her death, Semiramis was supposed to have turned into a dove; or, better still, to have been worshipped as a goddess. It was this identification with mysterious and seductive goddesses of the East, such as Astarte (or Ishtar), who first prowled along the edges of the Classical world and then invaded it, which was probably most important, in preserving her story, In this manner it was thrillingly carried away from the small patch of historical ground in which it had originally been rooted.

As for the mother–son relationship, Voltaire employed that in his play *Semiramis*, first performed in 1748 (and used by Rossini as the basis for his opera *Semiramide*). In so doing Voltaire gave the relationship a gloss which made it at once more tragic and more innocent. Once Semiramis had

> led her army and her people captive
> And spite of time, with more than magic art,
> Chained down the minds of men, the universe
> Astonished stood, and trembled at her feet . . .

Now Semiramis is doomed by her love for Arsaces (unknown to her, he is her own son) because love itself, not incest, will rob her of her ability to command her people and her army.

Nevertheless it is difficult to believe that when Voltaire dubbed Catherine the Great his 'Semiramis of the North' he had in mind the possibility of such an agonizing maternal dilemma on her part; surely it was the role of the triumphant female general and even more the out-of-hours employer of strong soldiery, which was the link between Semiramis and Catherine. Voltaire's Semiramis was the lascivious one described by Diodorus Siculus in the first century BC: 'what knight in her eye was the most goodly and personable man, him she would covertly choose out from all her army of people and disport her with him after her appetite . . .'⁴

Herodotus had more admiration for the bold Tomyris, Queen of the nomadic Massagetae (living in what is now eastern Iran) than he had for Semiramis. It was to Tomyris, as queen and general of the army, that Herodotus ascribed the death of Cyrus the Great, King of the Medes and Persians, in 529 BC preferring the account which makes a woman the agent of his fall to all the others. (The point has been made that in half the total mentions of women by Herodotus they are shown as 'actors who themselves determine the outcome of events'.) Tomyris was a widow, left to rule the Massagetae after her husband's death, and Cyrus' first effort to take over her territories was couched in an offer of marriage. Tomyris declined this: 'for the queen was well aware that he was wooing not herself but her dominions'.⁵

What was more, Tomyris then urged Cyrus to leave the Massagetae in peace. As she watched the bridges being built which would enable Cyrus' armies to cross the River Araxes and begin his assault against her people, she sent him a message urging him to desist, containing the not unreasonable plea: 'Rule your own people, and try to bear the sight of me ruling mine.' Unfortunately, as Tomyris herself admitted, peace could scarcely be the aim of the all-powerful Persian King, he who had within twenty years founded an empire based on conquest from the Aegean Sea to the Indus river. So Tomyris' next suggestion was that Cyrus should abandon his bridge-building and a meeting should be set up. Either the Massagetae would retreat three days' march from the river and Cyrus would cross, or Cyrus would retreat and the Massagetae would make the crossing.

According to Herodotus, Cyrus seriously considered this proposal and at a meeting of his chief officers it met with almost universal approval. The exception was Croesus the Lydian whose arguments ended tellingly (invoking the spectre of the Shame Syndrome): 'And apart from what I have already said, it would surely be an intolerable disgrace for Cyrus son of Cambyses to give ground before a woman.' So Croesus advocated crossing the river and getting the better of the Massagetae by a Glencoe-like strategy involving a banquet.

In the event the Persians would have done better to listen to the reasonable Tomyris than to the tricky Croesus. The latter's strategy led successfully in the first instance to the slaughter of a number of Massagetae, sated by the banquet, and the capture of Tomyris' son, Spargapises. This time the message sent back to Cyrus by Tomyris was as follows: 'Glutton as you are for blood, you have no cause to be proud of this day's work, which has no smack of soldierly courage.' She continued grimly: 'Give me back my son and get out of my country with your forces intact, and be content with your triumph over a third part of the Massagetae. If you refuse, I swear by the sun our master to give you more blood than you can drink, for all your gluttony.'

Tomyris saw to it that her vow was horribly fulfilled. The nomadic Queen swept down upon the Persians and after a bloody battle – 'which . . . I judge to have been more violent than any other fought between foreign nations', wrote Herodotus – the Massagetae succeeded in slaughtering the Persians, including Cyrus himself. Finding Spargapises had committed suicide in captivity, Tomyris had the dead body of Cyrus brought to her from the field, whereupon she pushed the head of the corpse into a skin which she had filled with human blood, saying, 'Though I have conquered you and live, yet you have ruined me by treacherously taking my son. See now – I fulfil my threat: you have your fill of blood.'

Yet for all Tomyris' courage and a bloodthirstiness in a measure at least justified, it is evident that her reputation survives merely as a footnote to that of Cyrus. Boccaccio, for example, commending her for her courage – she did not look for a place to hide 'like a fearful woman' when faced with the spectacle of Cyrus' army – gave a final verdict with which it is difficult to disagree: 'she was famous in proportion to the power of Cyrus'.[6] The Warrior Queen, whatever her qualities as a general or even as a human being, begins a long career of attachment to some male figure or figures of supreme reputation; she may challenge him successfully (as Tomyris to Cyrus) or she may fail gallantly in the attempt (as Boudica to the Romans) but she begins to be defined, unlike the war-goddess, by the connection: a refinement of the Appendage Syndrome, not in familial but in historical terms.

Fifty years after the death of Cyrus the Great, another brave queen accompanied another Persian king, Xerxes, to war against the Greeks and, although defeated at his side in the battle of Salamis, emerged from the contest with her reputation enhanced. It is true that something of Herodotus' partiality for Artemisia, Queen Regent of Halicarnassus, may be due to the fact that she was the local heroine, Herodotus himself springing from that same rocky promontory on the south Aegean shore (now the site of Bodrum in modern Turkey). Herodotus was born in 484 BC, that is to say he was only four years old at the time of the battle of Salamis; as a boy he listened to the tales of the men who had sailed with the famous Artemisia.[7] As a result Herodotus' anecdotal portrait of the Queen has a vividness and plausibility beyond mere local patriotism.

He began by admitting that it was 'a most strange and interesting thing' that Artemisia – a woman – should have taken part in the campaign against Greece. But he then went on to emphasize that it was not a mere fluke of inheritance that brought Artemisia to command. Of Cretan blood from her mother, Artemisia assumed power on the death of her Halicarnassan father Lygdamis: at first sight this is an example of Warrior Queen as Appendage, following the failure of the male line; but there was in fact a male heir available in the shape of Artemisia's grown-up son. So Artemisia's dashing expedition was due to her own force of character; or, as Herodotus put it, 'her own sprit of adventure and her manly courage were her only incentives'.

Furthermore Artemisia showed herself from the start of Xerxes' fatal naval campaign against the Greeks prudent as well as adventurous. It was Artemisia, alone of Xerxes' commanders, who suggested that the Persian King should learn the lesson of his recent defeat at the hands of the Greeks at Euboea, and not challenge the Greek naval power by putting to sea. Her advice was couched in apparently modest terms: 'The Greeks are as far superior to us in naval matters as men are to women', although she had begun by noting that it was her own courage and achievements at Euboea 'surpassed by none' which gave her the right to speak so boldly. She pointed out that if Xerxes rushed into another naval action, the ruin of his fleet might involve the ruin of his army as well.

Artemisia's intervention was heard with bated breath by the other members of Xerxes' council: her friends feared she had ruined herself, the jealous hoped that her sway over Xerxes would now be diminished. In the event Xerxes disregarded Artemisia's advice – he decided that the failure at Euboea had been due to his own absence, which had enabled his men to shirk their duty. But his high opinion of her perspicacity was at the same time confirmed.

What was more, Artemisia's conduct at Salamis, compared to that of Xerxes' male commanders, called forth the celebrated lament, 'My men have turned into women, my women into men.' It is the cry, an essential part of the Shame Syndrome, which will be heard again and again in the history of the Warrior Queen, down to the twentieth century, when Mrs Gandhi was described as 'the only man in the cabinet of old women' during her first year in office and the Labour politician George Brown called Mrs Thatcher 'the best man in the Tory Party'.[8]

Artemisia's escape from the scene of the naval engagement showed a special bravado. According to Herodotus, 'it was Ameinias who gave chase to Artemisia, and if he had known that Artemisia was on board, he would never have abandoned the chase until he had either taken her or been taken himself; for the Athenians resented the fact that a woman should appear in arms against them, and the ships' captains had received special orders about her, with the offer of a reward of 10,000 drachmae for anyone who captured her alive'.

Artemisia, faced with the problem of eluding Ameinias' trireme, adopted a radical solution. Instead of trying to engage Ameinias, she boldly rammed the ship of one of her own allies. The ruse succeeded. The Greeks assumed Artemisia's ship to be one of their own side and abandoned the chase. At the same time the ramming was noted from afar and brought to the attention of Xerxes himself with the words: 'Do you see, my lord, how well Artemisia is fighting? She has sunk an enemy ship.' For the Persians, like the Greeks, could not conceive of Artemisia ramming one of her own allies.

Artemisia rounded off the campaign, successful at least from the point of view of her own prestige, by giving Xerxes another sage piece of advice. She suggested that the Persian King should now leave his general Mardonius behind in the country to complete the design, since that was Mardonius' wish. 'If his design prospers and success attends his arms, it will be *your* work, master – for your slaves performed it. And even if things go wrong with him, it will be no great matter so long as you yourself are safe.' This time – since Artemisia's advice exactly coincided with his own inclinations – Xerxes followed it. And his admiration for Artemisia was greater than ever.

All in all, it is not difficult to sympathize with the verdict of John Aylmer in the sixteenth century. Put up to defending Queen Elizabeth I against the attacks of Calvin and Knox on female 'regiment' (government), he referred more than once to the story of Artemisia and Xerxes. Artemisia the woman, he pointed out, had shown more talent to rule than Xerxes the man.[9]

The trouble with this perception of the Warrior Queen as one whose behaviour and indeed whose whole career served as an implicit chastisement of the opposite sex was that it existed entirely in the moral sphere of the narrator. As Thomas Heywood observed in his seventeenth-century *Gynaekeion* – although the sentiment was universal from the time of the Greeks onwards – 'I know not better how to express the boldness of women, than by shewing you the fear of men, nor can I more plainly illustrate the valor of one sex than by putting you in mind the cowardice of another.'[10]

Bearing this in mind, the story of Cleopatra's treatment by the Romans in the century before Boudica and above all the story of her treatment as a would-be 'Queen of War' acts as a significant footnote to the history of pre-Boudican female warrior leaders. Where practical politics were concerned, no Warrior Queen could count on the kind of approval meted out by Herodotus to Artemisia in his character study of a woman at once sagacious and brave (beyond the capacity of all the surrounding contemporary males). Like other client rulers, or those designated as such by the Romans, she would be judged entirely by her usefulness to the advancement of the Roman cause (which, put simply, happened to be profitable overlordship of the known world). At the same time sexual licence attributed where possible to a Warrior Queen would be aimed as a barbed political arrow: where Cleopatra was concerned, it was convenient that Artemisia should be forgotten, Semiramis remembered.

Cleopatra VII – as she would become – was born in late 70 or early 69 BC, one of the six children of Ptolemy XII Auletes (the word means the Piper). Of these six, there were two girls older than Cleopatra, Cleopatra VI Tryphaena and Berenice IV; after Cleopatra came a fourth daughter Arsinoe and then two sons by Auletes' second wife, Ptolemy XIII and Ptolemy XIV, born in 61 and 59 BC respectively. There is some doubt about the identity of Cleopatra's mother, but Auletes' first wife Cleopatra V Tryphaena (mother of her two elder sisters) is the most likely choice.[11]

It is of course important to realize that Cleopatra came from a line of Hellenistic queens, something which should not be obscured by the exceptional fame with which literature has endowed her. Equally important is the truth about Cleopatra's blood and upbringing. Shakespeare's 'serpent of the old Nile' was in fact to all intents and purposes a Greek; she had Macedonian, Persian and Syrian blood as well as Greek, but her language was Greek. She had no Egyptian blood, although as an intelligent, well-educated woman she may possibly have spoken Egyptian. Cleopatra's Greek upbringing meant that she had been raised up in the knowledge of the great Hellenistic monarchies which had existed in the past: but she was also aware that these were now mere insubstantial memories, as Egypt had passed under Roman tutelage during the previous century. Cleopatra's father had been established as a kind of puppet monarch during the Roman dictatorship of Sulla; as a child Cleopatra might have known of the typically humiliating incident in which her own father was received by Cato as a course of laxatives were being administered to him.[12]

It is possible that Cleopatra co-ruled with her father for a period of weeks or months before the end of his life; at all events she was pronounced co-ruler with her ten-year-old brother Ptolemy XIII on Auletes' death in 51 BC. Such a union with her brother was a crucial step. Firstly, these repeated Ptolemaic marriages of brother and sister, whatever their genetic consequences, were intended to play upon the Egyptian devotion to their gods Osiris and Isis: the first-born children of the god of the earth and the goddess of the sky who married each other. The Ptolemies, as they enacted the roles of brother–husband and sister–wife, appealed to the patriotism of the Egyptians and at the same time emphasized their own divine origins as lawgivers.

Secondly, from the point of view of Cleopatra, as with her other female relatives, some kind of male ruler was essential, *de jure* if not *de facto* (the notion that these Hellenistic queens were ever considered *de jure* sole rulers cannot be upheld, even if their renown to say nothing of their strength of character far outstripped that of their fainéant brothers).[13] Cleopatra VII was exceptional in that, as effective ruler in her own right, her head did actually appear alone on bronze coins inside Egypt. Her female predecessors' heads had only appeared occasionally on gold and silver coins – and even then in the guise of Isis.

The picture we do have is of a Cleopatra who was not only strong-minded but ambitious enough to have her own conception of empire, involving the restoration of the glorious Ptolemaic dominion which had once extended as far as Syria and Palestine. As in the case of another celebrated *femme fatale* of history, Mary Queen of Scots, a close inspection of Cleopatra's career reveals far more concentration on power politics and far less self-indulgent dalliance than wistful popular imagination cares to admit. Whether beautiful or not (she has a heavy if sultry look to the modern eye), Cleopatra certainly understood how to make the best use of her fascinating femininity. After a series of intrigues led to her disposition in 49 BC, Cleopatra set her sights upon the strong man of Rome, Julius Caesar, appreciating that he had the power to restore her.

Plutarch tells the celebrated story of her arrival at Caesar's palace in a sleeping bag rolled up: 'This little trick of Cleopatra's, which showed her provocative impudence, is said to have been the first thing about her which captivated Caesar, and, as he grew to know her better, he was overcome by her charm and arranged that she and her brother should be reconciled and share the throne of Egypt together.'[14] (But Ptolemy XIII was in fact subsequently defeated with Caesar's help, and put to death, leaving Cleopatra to share the throne officially with her younger brother Ptolemy XIV.

The birth of a boy known as Caesarion in 47 BC, after Caesar had left Egypt, further strengthened Cleopatra's hand in view of her theoretical need for a male co-ruler, and her practical need for a submissive one. Julius Caesar was generally thought to be the father of the child, as his name indeed indicates, but later, by officially ascribing paternity to her brother Ptolemy XIV, Cleopatra brought the boy within the necessary network of the Ptolemaic royal family. After Ptolemy XIV had been disposed of, like Ptolemy XIII (and at another date Cleopatra's sister Arsinoe), Cleopatra was able in time to establish herself as co-sovereign with her own son as Ptolemy xv Caesar. This other 'little trick' of Cleopatra's, whatever its 'impudence', has nothing particularly languorous about it.

Meanwhile as Caesar's mistress, Cleopatra journeyed to Rome, a visit either underplayed or excoriated by the Romans in later years. Cicero's description of her sojourn in Rome belonged to the latter category: 'I detest Cleopatra,' he wrote, 'and the insolence of the queen . . . when she was in her villa across the river [i.e. the Tiber] I cannot mention without great indignation.'[15] It was a taste of what was to come. At the time Cleopatra was saluted by Caesar with a golden statue of herself in the temple of Venus Genetrix, the publicly proclaimed ancestress of Caesar's own Julian family. She was still living there in 44 BC when Caesar's assassination put an end to her political hopes – from that direction.

The rise of Mark Antony after the defeat of Caesar's assassins at Philippi in 42 BC, presented Cleopatra with another opportunity to exert her wiles in the interest of gratifying her territorial ambitions. She arrived to greet him in Tarsus in Asia Minor by barge up the River Cydnus, a scene originally described by Plutarch that lives forever at the pen of Shakespeare. Outwardly, Cleopatra appeared more as a goddess than as a potential mistress. Plutarch wrote: 'the word spread on every side that Aphrodite had come to revel with Dionysus for the happiness of Asia'.

For Cleopatra herself, although Aphrodite was held in certain circles to be a mother goddess (which was useful), it was Isis who proved throughout her reign the most convenient point of identification. In the East, the cult of Isis stretched back for at least two thousand years: here was the national divinity of Egypt, the Great Mother of all the gods and of nature itself, the equivalent of Dionysus: except that the cult of Isis, which could be followed by both men and women, presupposed the equality of the female sex. Only one Ptolemaic creed connected with the cult has come down to us but it is a remarkable one from the point of view of a putative Warrior Queen: 'I am Isis, the Mistress of every land . . . I gave and ordained Laws for men, which no one is able to change . . . I am she that rises in the Dogstar, she who is called Goddess by women . . . I made man strong . . . I am the queen of war. I am the queen of the thunderbolt. I stir up the sea and calm it. I am the rays of the Sun.'[16] At one point, not only did Cleopatra project herself as the New Isis, but she projected her lover Antony as the New Osiris: not an agreeable concept to Antony's political enemies at Rome.

Even more threatening from the point of view of those hostile to the renewal of the Ptolemaic empire were such words as these, taken from the so-called Sibylline books, a corpus of prophetic literature, probably written at the height of Cleopatra's power:

> But when the Tenth Generation goes down to Hades
> There comes a Woman's great power . . .
> And then the whole wide world under a woman's hand . . .

Soon Rome, the 'delicate gilded voluptuous maiden', would be at 'a mistress' stern command'.[17]

Cleopatra's territorial fortunes certainly prospered with Antony under her sway. Not only were lands handed over to her far into Asia Minor but her personal wealth was increased with the gift of the Nabatean Arab kingdom, enabling her to exploit its bitumen resources. It has been suggested that new coins issued jointly with Ptolemy xv Caesar (her son) commemorated this fortunate new development.[18] At the same time, the name of Cleopatra's son by Antony, born in 40 BC, Alexander Helios, pointed to the cult of the sun; his twin sister Cleopatra Selene being similarly linked to the moon goddess.

At the Donations of Alexandria of 34 BC, by which little Alexander Helios was to rule Armenia, his two-year-old brother Ptolemy Philadelphus the lands to the west, and his sister Cleopatra Selene Cyrene, all the children were dressed in suitable national garb – Alexander in the traditional high royal cap of the ancient Persian monarchs. When Antony visited Athens, it was the statue of Cleopatra, dressed in the robes of Isis, which the Greeks erected on the Acropolis.

The Roman attitude to the New Isis (and the new Osiris) was very different. As political opposition to Antony on the part of his brother-in-law Octavian hardened, Cleopatra was increasingly depicted as an unpleasant Eastern siren who had seduced the Roman Antony, in order to play out a life of debauchery with him far from his Roman duties (and his wife Octavia). Octavian proclaimed to the Roman people, on the basis of Antony's will, which he seized from the temple of the Vestal Virgins, not only that Antony had given away Roman possessions to Cleopatra, but also that he intended to found a new dynasty with her, based on Alexandria, not Rome. It was thus the destiny of Octavian (the future Caesar Augustus) to contain her: 'as swiftly as the hawk follows the feeble dove', wrote Roman Horace with an air of satisfaction not lacking in vindictiveness for all the trouble Cleopatra had caused. 'So he sailed forth to bind this fatal prodigy in chains.'[19]

How different, how very different, at least in the popular imagination, was the sensuous and commanding Cleopatra from modest Octavia at home, Antony's lawful Roman wife! Octavia's admirable disposition encouraged her to plead for mercy where possible; ultimately she would bring up the children of Antony and Cleopatra (the surest test not only of an admirable but of a charitable nature). As for Fulvia, that vigorous Roman matron, Antony's previous wife, this was how Plutarch described her: not content to rule a husband who had no ambition for public life, her desire was 'to govern those who governed or to command a commander-in-chief'.[20] But Fulvia's ambitions were also alien to Cleopatra, who was herself 'the Queen of War'.

The winter of 33/32 BC was spent by Antony and Cleopatra together at Ephesus. In this period of gathering storm, the perpetual presence of Cleopatra not only at banquets but at military conferences was criticized by the Roman Ahenobarbus (another character gruffly familiar to us from Shakespeare). While Ahenobarbus wished in vain for Antony to send Cleopatra away, it was left to another Roman, Canidius Crassus, to point out another aspect to the situation. Not only had Cleopatra contributed a great deal from her own treasury to the expenses of the war (of the five hundred warships under Antony's command, Cleopatra had provided two hundred) but she had also ruled a great kingdom without effective aid for many years – and was by no means inferior in intelligence to the other kings Antony counted as his allies.

When Octavian formally declared war against Cleopatra (not Antony) at the end of 32, he also chose to direct his most vicious attacks against the 'licentious' Egyptian Queen, rather than against the man who might easily have been regarded as a treacherous Roman. Antony's subjection to Cleopatra was declared to be incomprehensible (here was the Voracity Syndrome at work, with a vengeance). The poet Propertius made of Cleopatra 'that courtesan obscene . . . that worst of stigmas branded on the Royal race of Macedon' who 'dared pit against our Jupiter, Her god Anubis, half a cur'. In another line, almost risible to modern ears in its disgust, Cleopatra was accused of longing on 'Tarpeia's rock to set, The effeminate mosquito net'.[21]

This dichotomy between the Cleopatra of independent character and independent wealth described by Canidius Crassus, and the 'courtesan obscene' of Propertius persisted until the very end of the great adventure shared with Antony. It is even possible to argue that the sea battle at Actium in September 31 BC which terminated it, was justifiable, if Cleopatra's view that a land battle would have ensured the loss of her ships be accepted. As for Cleopatra's presence at the scene of the battle (the Romans, like Napoleon later, thought a battle was no place for a woman), that too is explicable if one accepts that she was needed as the figurehead to her own troops; alternatively that her personal safety was guaranteed more easily there than if she had been left on shore.

More starkly, Horace put forward the Roman view that Cleopatra was the 'wild Queen' who had plotted 'ruin to the Empire'. So Cleopatra's reputation was trampled into the mire by

the Romans, much as Shakespeare has Cleopatra predict to her
waiting-woman Iras at the end of the play that the two of them
will be turned into puppets:

> The quick comedians
> Extemporally will stage us, and present
> Our Alexandrian revels. Antony
> Shall be brought drunken forth, and I shall see
> Some squeaking Cleopatra boy my greatness
> I' the posture of a whore.[22]

Like his fellow Romans, Horace ignored the possibility that
Cleopatra might legitimately have ambitions of her own – for
another kind of empire, under the domain of a Ptolemaic
Warrior Queen. The Roman treatment of Cleopatra in this
respect may be profitably contrasted with that meted out to
Dynamis of Bosphorus whose name means 'she who must be
obeyed' but who is sometimes known as the Bosphoran
Cleopatra.[23] Dynamis' husband King Asander had been recognized as ruler of the kingdom of the Cimmerian Bosphorus by
both Antony and Octavian, Dynamis herself being the daughter
of the late king. In about 17 BC, however, a certain Scribonius,
alleged to be Dynamis' lover, instigated a revolt against the
now elderly sovereign. Whatever Dynamis' part in the original
uprising, she indubitably threw in her lot with Scribonius against
her husband, leaving the aged Asander (he was said to be over
ninety) to starve himself to death. Dynamis' next step was to
assume control of the country herself, her own descent from
Mithridates being an important factor in bolstering up her
position. The evidence of the coins, showing her head alone,
indicated that Scribonius was not invited to share the throne,
even if he shared the bed.

Such a revolution in the Bosphoran kingdom could not be
regarded with equanimity by the Romans, notably by Marcus
Agrippa, Governor of Jerusalem. The kingdom's position both as
a bulwark against the wild men surrounding it to the north, east

and west, and as a gateway for the empire's supplies, demanded a stable Roman-controlled government.

Polemo, King of neighbouring Pontus, was accordingly sent into the field, having been promised the hand of Queen Dynamis if he managed to subdue the rebel Bosphorans. Reducing the Bosphorans to a state of submission was not difficult in that they had already thoughtfully put Scribonius to death of their own accord. Pontus duly received the kingdom of Bosphorus and he duly married Dynamis.

But Dynamis' story was not to be so tamely concluded. Fleeing from what proved to be an unhappy marriage, she raised a fresh revolt, this time against Polemo, with the help of a Sarmatian tribe. Dynamis now felt herself free to wed a young Sarmatian named Aspurgus. With his help, a series of military campaigns ended with the victory of Dynamis over Polemo, and the death of the latter at the hands of Aspurgus in 8 BC. Still, Dynamis could not rest easy until she had been accepted by Augustus Caesar and his representative Agrippa.

Once this was established, her chequered past, in both moral and political terms, proved no bar to her acceptance by the Romans. So Dynamis became a Roman vassal, receiving the title of 'friend of the Roman people'. Although her head now disappeared from Bosphoran coins, being replaced by those of Augustus and Agrippa, Dynamis unlike Cleopatra lived to a ripe old age, dying in AD 7 or 8.

It was Anchises, father of Aeneas, whom Virgil had prophesy the special destiny of the Romans, when Aeneas encountered him in the underworld: 'You, Roman, must remember that you have to guide the nations by your authority, for this is to be your skill, to graft tradition on to peace, to shew mercy to the conquered, and to wage war until the haughty are brought low.'[24] Of the two striking Warrior Queens whom the Romans encountered in the first century BC, Dynamis' fate illustrated the mercy shown to the conquered regardless of sex or behaviour, when convenient from the point of view of security. But Cleopatra, by placing herself unlike Dynamis in the category of 'the haughty', received a very different kind of treatment. Her fate was that of those whose ambitions or pretensions were inconvenient to the mighty Roman Empire.

It was a lesson to be learned again ninety years after Cleopatra's death by another Warrior Queen, Boudica.

CHAPTER FOUR

Iceni: this Powerful Tribe

~

We had not defeated this powerful tribe in battle, since
they had voluntarily become our allies.

TACITUS ON THE ICENI, AD 47

Boudica, like most Warrior Queens, was royal by birth and ruled over an aristocracy. The later Iron Age society in which she lived might be 'barbarian' by the standards of Rome – the Latin word means literally strange or foreign, not savage as it has come to mean in modern usage – but it was certainly not anarchic. Furthermore, she lived in a period of transition when Roman influences had already been brought to bear upon parts of England as a result of military invasion, commercial dealings and finally military occupation for a generation before her uprising.

This is not to say that the Iceni, the tribe of which she became the leader on her husband's death, were in the forefront of Romanization. There were more sophisticated groups to be found in the middle of the first century AD, using the word sophisticated to denote such matters as literacy and style of living, whose geographical position had brought them into closer contact with the Romans.

Geography indeed plays an important part in the story of the Iceni as it does in that of Boudica herself. The Iceni territories, broadly speaking, encompassed modern Norfolk and north Suffolk, an area which even today can give an impression of rural seclusion, vast tracts of land whose inhabitants are not in immediate daily touch with any metropolis. That natural disposition of the terrain which leaves East Anglia in a sense out on its own large limb was obviously an even more potent factor in preserving Iceni independence in the Iron Age.

Despite this caveat, it would be quite wrong to regard Boudica herself as some kind of violent savage: a woad-stained and shrieking animal. Furthermore, since her behaviour at times can fairly be considered violent, it would be wrong to regard that behaviour also as being merely the mindless outbreak of a female ruffian. Boudica did exist; she did spring from a particular society; her conduct, whether heroic or reprehensible, was the product of that society and its standards.

The first recorded mention of the Iceni tribe occurs, almost certainly, in Caesar's report on his second invasion of Britain, roughly a hundred years before Boudica's rebellion. Julius Caesar's first invasion, in 55 BC, had not taken him across the Thames. The following year however he made the crossing, and following the defeat of a British overlord named Cassivellaunus, received the submission of a number of tribes. Foremost among these were the Trinovantes – Camulodunum (Colchester) was a centre associated with their name – and it was in fact the appeal of the Trinovantes to Caesar for protection against Cassivellaunus' dominion which had provoked the latter's final defeat. The Trinovantes' submission was the obvious corollary to their appeal; the five other tribes who also submitted presumably judged it prudent to do so. Among their names are listed the Cenimagni – 'the great Iceni'. (This is to assume, as is generally done, that the Cenimagni are to be equated with the Iceni: the mention of 'the great Iceni' may of course postulate the existence of another tribe, the lesser Iceni, who did not submit.)[1]

Then Caesar departed for the second time, and this time he did not come again. As the years passed, the British tribes must have hoped or even believed that he had taken away his doughty Roman legionaries for ever. The Iceni at least sank back into that kind of historical obscurity to which lack of literary evidence can consign a whole people for a whole century: 'the world forgetting, by the world forgot.'[*] [3]

---

[*] In local British terms, the river name Itchen may be related to the tribal name Iceni, but Ixworth or Ickenham are not thought to be so related.[2]

Even when in AD 43 the Emperor Claudius instigated a fresh invasion – which as it proved developed into four hundred years of occupation – the name of the Iceni did not immediately recur. It is true that there are those eleven mysterious 'kingdoms' – mysterious because unnamed – associated with the Arch erected to Claudius to celebrate his triumph. According to the inscription, the Emperor 'received the surrender of eleven kings of Britain, defeated without any loss', as well as being 'the first to bring barbarian peoples across the Ocean under the sway of the Roman people'. Quite possibly, among these 'kingdoms' (or tribes) whose rulers surrendered are to be found the Iceni.[4]

Nevertheless, the next specific reference to the Iceni occurs in Tacitus' account of their first rebellion. Four years after the Claudian invasion, the Romans, under their governor Aulus Plautius, were pushing north and west. There is some dispute concerning their intentions, fuelled by an obscure text in Tacitus. Did they intend, by reducing 'the whole territory as far as the Trent and Severn', to establish that line of defence now known as the Fosse Way as a kind of frontier? Or did they intend to pursue the possibility of further conquest?[5] Whatever their future plans, the Romans proceeded to deal with those tribes left behind by this advance in a manner which was summary if not sagacious.

For the incoming Governor of Britain, Ostorius Scapula, who arrived in 47, took the radical step of disarming his own allies. He did so in the interests of protecting his rear. Ostorius found himself dealing with escalating guerrilla warfare on the modern Welsh borders, the raiders from beyond the Roman lines being encouraged in their depredations by the charismatic British leader Caratacus. Meanwhile to the north, the attitude of that sprawling federation of tribes, the Brigantes, remained uncertain. Nevertheless the indignation of the British 'allies' to the east thus disarmed was potent: they were after all being deprived of their weapons, in an essentially bellicose world, in anticipation of a rebellion which had yet to take place.

Among the disarmed peoples, there was one whose reaction was especially bitter: the Iceni. 'We had not defeated this powerful tribe in battle,' wrote Tacitus, 'since they had voluntarily become our allies.'[6] It was under the leadership of the Iceni that the neighbouring tribes now rose up against the Romans. The rebellion, generally placed in about AD 49/50, was not successful. The Romans put it down with ease, although Tacitus noted that the British comported themselves bravely to the last, performing 'prodigies of valour' even when there was 'no way out'. The Iceni did however survive as a quasi-independent body: that is to say, they remained as a client-kingdom of Rome, their leader as client-king having specific obligations as well as rights.

It is at about this point that Prasutagus emerges as client-king of the Iceni. No date is known for certain beyond the fact that when he died in 59 or 60 he had been ruling for a long time. Maybe he was already ruling over one branch of the Iceni in 43, and was placed at the head of the other branch – assuming there were two – in 49. Maybe he simply emerged in 49 in the wake of the rebellion as one capable of leading his people in peace. All of this is speculation. What is important from the point of view of this study is the fact of Prasutagus' marriage. At some point equally unclear, but almost certainly before the AD 49 rebellion, Prasutagus had married a woman of royal birth called Boudica.[7]

Already this, the first incontrovertible mention of the Iceni, has painted a picture of a tribe both vigorous and resentful, their voluntary submission humiliatingly disregarded in the wider interests of Roman policy; one, furthermore, capable of showing courage even in despair. In the light of subsequent events, it is a significant image. And another image may perhaps be added to it: that of a young woman – a queen – with her own memories of Roman injustice, revolt and suppression.

What sort of people were they, the Iceni? First of all, it is important to understand their Celtic heritage. That is to say, a thousand years before, their ancestors had formed part of the great Celtic world spread across Northern Europe.[8] It is a heritage which marks the Iceni, despite the fact that by AD 49 their client-kingdoms existed on the very frontiers of the

Romanized and apparently settled world. But then it was a powerful heritage, the Classical writers displaying a remarkable unanimity in commenting upon the characteristics of the Celts from the German forests to the sandy stretches of Spain. (They wrote about them either as Galli – 'the Gauls' – or as Keltoi, presumably how such people described themselves.)

We are of course dependent on the views of these outsiders since the Celts themselves, as Caesar noted of the Gauls, considered it 'improper to entrust their studies to writing'. It is true that there is 'presumptive evidence' for the import of writing materials into Britain before the Claudian invasion. In Britain in the years before the Boudican revolt, the unwritten Celtic language was gradually being replaced by the Romans' Latin for purposes of administration and commerce. In the same way, during this period of transition, the native spoken language was being permeated by Latin.[9] Nevertheless the basic culture of the Celts, being an unwritten one, remains destined to be observed from outside, rather than delineated from within.

Above all the Celts were brave: those prodigies of valour noted by Tacitus in 49 were customary, not unique. Like many (but not all) brave people, the Celts also loved the fight itself, dashing joyously and frequently into the fray, laughing and shouting their way either to bloody death or to an equally bloody victory. The traveller and Stoic Strabo, who died in about AD 21, described the Celts in his *Geographica*: the whole race, he wrote, was war-mad, both high-spirited and quick for battle, although otherwise simple and not ill-mannered.[10]

With courage went recklessness. It was, Strabo continued, easy to outwit them, since they were always ready to face danger 'even if they have nothing on their side but their own strength and courage'. The Romans noted their use of single combat upon occasion, the contestants flinging themselves down from their chariots (which would actually be light affairs of bentwood, no knives on the wheels, very different from the chariot supporting Boadicea on the Thames-side sculpture).[11] They also observed that the Celts fought naked, something they were well equipped to do; for this was a robust, well-muscled race who placed much emphasis on physical fitness. Furthermore, the Celts, as perceived by the Classical writers and depicted in Classical sculpture, were not only strong but tall and big-boned, with thick, flowing fair or reddish hair (in contrast to the modern idea of the 'Celtic type' as being small, neat and dark-haired).

Loud noises – trumpets and clappers in the form of animal heads – also attended the conflicts of the Celts. Noise, whether the braying of trumpets, the sounding of clappers or music itself at their frequent feastings, was indeed a universal taste among them. Such hospitable feasts would also be marked by lavish imbibing, either leading to singing or concurrent with it: drink being another universal taste. Wine for the aristocrats and wheaten beer for the rest was the custom, the whole spiced with cumin. Vast loving cups would be handed round, and although the sips taken might be small, Strabo added, 'they do it rather frequently'.

Another passion was for rich personal ornament, something which would now be termed conspicuous consumption perhaps, but was then, in Strabo's opinion at least, part of their general naïve boastfulness. Heavy gleaming gold, twisted and chased, was the best material of all: gold round the neck, gold bracelets on the arms were common to high-born men and women alike. Brooches were enamelled, cloaks were fastened with imposing buckles. Even in war, this passion for ornamentation was not subdued but extended to the helmets of the charioteers and to weapons such as shields. Colour was not ignored: clothing (like Boudica's cloak) was generally stained and dyed in a variety of hues and stripes, making a kind of early tartan.

Starting about five hundred years before the time of Boudica, some of these fighting, singing, drinking, gold-bedecked Celts migrated across the English Channel from what are now the Low Countries to East Anglia. These were the ancestors of the Iceni. The first Celtic settlers who brought the practice of iron smelting were comparatively humble folk. Then in about 150 BC the warlords of the Marne Valley followed, bringing with them their chariots and their ponies (Iron Age horses were only about ten or eleven hands high).[12] Further migrations of so-called Belgic people – the Belgae from North Gaul – are still the subject of dispute, just as the distinction between Celts and Belgic people is itself blurred; but if the southern neighbours of the Iceni – the Trinovantes – were in some manner Belgic, it is the consensus of opinion that the Iceni in their geographic isolation remained 'Celtic', even if some 'Belgic' influences can be discerned as the century wore on.[13]

Whatever these distinctions, certain it is there followed in the first century BC and the years up to the Claudian invasion of AD 43, that flowering of Iron Age civilization and British Celtic art to which recent archaeological finds bear such eloquent witness. Many of the most significant finds have been made in Iceni territory: the Brecklands, for example, an area of forestry and heather and marsh lying between Bury St Edmunds and Norwich, and in northern coastal areas near the Wash. (It is the pattern of archaeological finds, following the cleavage in the terrain, and in its turn providing the pattern of Iceni settlement, which gives some substance to the idea that there may have been two Iceni tribes, the greater and the lesser.)[14]

Many of these finds testify to the fact that this was a society dominated by the horse and, by extension, the chariot: the rich bridle-bits and bronze nave-bands, a charioteer's cap found at Snettisham. The coins of the Iceni are stamped with galloping horses, legs prancing, manes flowing wildly (like the luxuriant locks of their masters enshrined in Classical sculpture). As a result this society, ruled over by the horse-mad, as well as war-mad, chieftains, has been compared to that of other ancient chivalric orders, such as the Samurai of Japan or even the warriors of Homer.[15]

Not only the arts of war – enamelled scabbards and shields – called for the skills of the Celtic craftsmen: a style of living which may even be termed gracious, is revealed by the appearance, both intricate and exquisite, of certain domestic artefacts. Much fine metalwork including dolphin and thistle brooches was discovered in a hoard at Santon in north Norfolk. Moreover if nothing else of late Iron Age society had survived except its decorated bronze mirrors, its sophistication and artistic sense would still have been amply demonstrated. Sir Cyril Fox wrote lyrically of the 'perfection of harmony between hand and eye' which these north Celtic craftsmen displayed in the creation of the mirrors, their 'masterly and apparently effortless technique'[16] – words which are even outstripped by the objects themselves. Once again, Iceni graves have provided richly of these mirrors.

It is however in the massive gold torcs or necklaces (from the Latin *torquis*) that the confident and aristocratic nature of Iceni society is perhaps best understood. Unlike the bronze mirrors, the powerful beauty of these magnificent objects is ill conveyed even by photographs, let alone in words. Gold – the Celtic favourite – is by far the most popular material, although torcs of bronze and even silver are known. Their precise function will probably never be perfectly understood: Boudica will be described as wearing one round her neck as she harangued her troops on the eve of battle. Yet those who have tried on a torc, even very briefly, speak of the extraordinary weight (those in the Snettisham hoard, to be discussed below, vary between 1,000 and 858 grams).[17] Some are more flexible than others – some are made of gold strands, some tubular with the external diameters between nine and seven and a half inches; but none is flexible and light enough to make long-term wearing anything but a burden. In particular, the possibility of actually fighting in torcs, at any rate those such as have survived in the Norfolk and Suffolk hoards, must be seriously called in question.

Did the torc then have some more ritual function? That is to say, did the Iceni chiefs merely wear them on state occasions when the weight would have to be endured in the interests of majesty, as a British sovereign endures the heavy weight of the Coronation regalia – the crown weighs over 2,000 grams – once in his or her lifetime? A declaration of war on Boudica's part would count as such a state occasion. Perhaps the torc was in fact a votive object which was housed in a sacred place, round the neck of an idol, when not in public use.

Two separate sets of torcs have been exposed by chance since the Second World War either within the main area of late Iron Age Iceni settlement at Snettisham near Hunstanton on the north-west Norfolk coast (1948/50) or contiguous to it, at Ipswich (1968/70).* The Snettisham Treasure, five hoards deposited some time between 25 BC and AD 10, was possibly the stock-in-trade of a metalsmith plying his wares from the south, or possibly Iceni loot after a profitable visit to their neighbours, the Trinovantes. The Ipswich torcs, whose extent suggests a gold-smith's workshop, are so similar in style that it has been suggested they originally came from north-west Norfolk.[18] If the precise significance of a torc is mysterious, the general significance of such a resplendent and indeed ostentatious object is not: a wealthy local dynasty.

In contrast to the torcs, the houses of the Iceni would indeed have a 'barbarous' look to modern eyes. But this is to misunder-stand the nature of Celtic society, where domestic comfort, as for example the incoming Romans understood it, was simply not an objective. The houses of the Iceni would have been those circular Iron Age structures with high, sloping roofs which to us now have an African look. (However, a 1973 experiment in recon-struction, the Butser Ancient Farm Project – the 'Maiden Castle' House – has revealed the durability of these round-houses compared to an African hut: their skilful building methods surviving the storms and rigours of British winters in a way the latter could never do.)[19] An ordinary house would be about fifty feet across, with a central fire. The palace of the Iceni would have consisted of a much larger dwelling – a great hall – constructed along the same lines and smaller outlying round-houses.

But no trace of Prasutagus' palace, and by extension that of Boudica herself, has yet been found. The most likely area for such a discovery is around Thetford. Excavations in the early 1980s at Gallows Hill, near Thetford, raised hopes, before the absence of

---

* A collection of torcs can be seen in the British Museum (from the Snettisham hoard) and in the Ipswich Museum (from the finds made locally).

all domestic detritus inevitable on the site of a palace dashed them again. The Thetford site is now thought to be some form of temple.[20] In the absence of a reliable finding, it is not only the particular situation of Boudica's palace which remains in doubt, but also, more generally, the pre-Roman tribal centre of the Iceni.

When the Roman soldiers were asked to take part in the Claudian invasion of 43, they waxed indignant. This was asking them to carry on a campaign 'outside the limits of the known world'.[21] It was actually true that the world they encountered within Britain both looked and was very different from their own – thatched round-houses in contrast to the Roman house of brick and tile. The lives of Celtic women were also very different from those of the Roman ladies who increasingly accompanied the occupying troops: while the notion of actual Celtic matriarchy has been dismissed, the women of the Iceni who looked into those exquisitely decorated bronze mirrors led the freer kind of tribal life in which the constraints imposed upon women by Roman law were quite unknown. A Roman female, having no rights at law herself, was from birth to death the property of her male relations.[22]

Roman society has been described as 'essentially a man's world'.[23] This was certainly not true of Celtic society. Not only law but religion, and religious attitudes to the sexes, were important areas of distinction. Women were excluded from the Mithraic religion which was spreading via the Roman armies across the empire. No such exclusion was ever contemplated where the Celts were concerned, a society still haunted by the powerful goddesses discussed in Chapter Two. There is every reason to believe that the priestly caste of the Celts, the Druids, included women as well as men.[24] Boudica's ability to summon up the character of priestess – or even goddess – on the eve of battle was to be an important factor where her war leadership was concerned: a capacity quite outside the experience of a Roman woman, however grand her status.

Caesar describes the entire Celtic people as being 'exceedingly given to religious superstition': that again was written from the

Roman point of view. Another way of putting it would be to stress the profoundly religious nature of Celtic society, with every grove and stream and well inhabited by its own deity, and the 'otherworld' ever present in the Celtic mind. In particular the human head in every form, from ornamental depiction to the skull of the enemy, has been described as being as central to the Celtic religion as the sign of the Cross (referring to the central act of the Crucifixion) in Christian contexts.[25]

To the Celts, the head was literally the godhead, the symbol of divinity or the centre of the human soul. The heads of their enemies, decapitated, took on symbolic importance. Livy wrote of the Gallic horsemen 'with heads hanging at their horses' breasts, or fixed on with their lances, and singing their customary song of triumph'. According to Strabo, the heads of 'enemies of high repute' were then embalmed in cedar-oil and exhibited to strangers; even if 'an equal weight of gold' was offered to ransom them, the Celts would refuse.[26] It is clear from this alone that the Celtic pre-occupation with the head cannot be equated, for example, with the mediaeval display of executed criminals' heads and limbs. It was numinous, not admonitory, in origin.

To the Romans, however, the zest with which Celts exhibited these severed treasures was not so much symbolic as revolting. It aroused the kind of disgust in the Roman breast which so-called superior civilizations have always reserved for the religious practices of those they designate – by right of conquest – to be inferior. Nevertheless, for all the Roman repulsion, this – deified groves, chanting priestesses as well as priests, and decapitated heads – was the religion which animated Boudica, as the Romans would discover to their cost when the conquerors were abruptly transformed into the conquered.

With the Iceni successfully subdued – as it seemed – the Roman action after 49 moved away from East Anglia back to the north and west. Here Caratacus still posed a threat: 'his many undefeated battles – and even many victories', wrote Tacitus, 'had made him pre-eminent among British chieftains'. His were the classical resources of the guerrilla leader, since 'his deficiency in strength was compensated by superior cunning and topographical knowledge'.[27]

The more northerly Brigantes were however soon defeated, as the Iceni had been, and after the deaths of a few 'peace-breakers' the rest were pardoned. Not only did this obviate the danger of a combination between the Brigantes and the 'exceptionally stubborn' Silures of modern Wales, it also presented Rome with a large and friendly client-kingdom across a wide spread of northern territories. Ironically enough, in view of subsequent events among the Iceni, this client-kingdom was ruled not by a client-king but by a queen: Cartimandua. The name Cartimandua, appropriately enough in this horse-haunted world, means 'Sleek Pony' – the kind of pony used to draw a chariot. This particular 'Sleek Pony' may well have been among those unnamed tribal monarchs who submitted to Claudius in 43, since she was clearly an established client-leader by the date of Caratacus' defeat.[28]

Even Caratacus could not hold out forever against the Roman legions. Vanquished at last in 51, he fled north to Cartimandua and the Brigantes (or else was captured by the Queen's trick – there are two different accounts). 'But the defeated have no refuge', wrote Tacitus. He might have added: when that refuge is under Roman protection. Caratacus was duly handed over by Queen Cartimandua, bound hand and foot, in order to appear as the centrepiece of Claudius' triumph at Rome. The client-queen had thus successfully 'furnished what was needed' by the Romans.[29]

Brigantian peace-at-a-price did not last long. Cartimandua's consort Venutius, also of royal blood, headed a revolt against her.[30] At first Cartimandua was able to survive by another of her cunning tricks, for she 'astutely trapped' Venutius' relatives. But then Venutius organized outside support. Tacitus is frank about the reason for this support: Cartimandua's enemies 'infuriated and goaded by fears of feminine rule, invaded her kingdom with a force of picked warriors'. Rome was obliged to come to her support, and it was with Rome's help that Cartimandua was able to remain upon her client-throne.

There is a parallel to be drawn here between Cartimandua and Queen Dynamis of Bosphorus. (But Cartimandua's capacity for survival in troubled times allied, not coincidentally, to a capacity for intrigue entitles her to be considered as the first-century Queen Elizabeth, if Boudica's dramatic end qualifies her perhaps to be its Mary Queen of Scots.) It is evident that whatever the Brigantian nobles may have felt, the Romans had no objection to 'humiliating feminine rule' so long as it suited their particular brand of power politics. The next stage of Cartimandua's story was however closer to that of Cleopatra then Dynamis. Some nine years after Boudica's rebellion, Cartimandua exercised what she clearly thought to be a queen's right to change her mind and acquired a new consort. She swapped the semi-royal Venutius for his armour-bearer Vellocatus. Tacitus, implicitly making the Queen part of the Voracity Syndrome, presents this as being due to lust: *'libido reginae'*. But it has been suggested that Cartimandua may actually have lusted after something very different: political support against Venutius. Once again Cartimandua was rescued by her Roman allies, although this time she did not survive on the throne itself, but was peacefully retired in favour of the *de facto* rule of Venutius.

It had been a long reign. In the extent of her territories and the power she wielded, Cartimandua can be compared to that celebrated southern client-king, Cogidubnus, builder of Fishbourne Palace, near Chichester. It is interesting therefore that Tacitus feels obliged to reflect on Cartimandua's *'libido'* and to treat the episode as a moral issue. (I. A. Richmond pointed out the irony of this in a lecture to Somerville College in 1953 – then as now an all-female institution – 'when the matrimonial experiments of the Julio-Claudian house and senatorial families in general are recalled'.)[31]

Furthermore the subsequent popular reputation of Cartimandua, obeying that rule which links sexuality to the Warrior Queen where possible, has concentrated on her adulterous aspect.

Ubaldini, in that history of illustrious women presented to Queen Elizabeth I, referred to Cartimandua in this fashion: 'she was a warlike woman and her way of acting was an example to the women of her country of how to be licentious, even if they were not born princesses'. Milton, writing a hundred years later in his *History of Britain* (when there was no queen regnant on the throne) was coarser. Cartimandua's military action was described as 'the Rebellion of an adulteress against her husband'. Her subjects were praised for siding with Venutius, since they thus displayed their detestation of 'so foul a fact' (the adultery); at the same time they rid themselves of 'the uncomeliness of their subjection to the Monarchy of a Woman'.[32]

This is to anticipate. The contemporary relevance of Cartimandua's lofty position and long reign with regard to Boudica is of a different nature. Tacitus described female leadership as something known among the Britons as opposed to the Romans, for example, where of course it was not: *neque enim sexum in imperiis discernunt* (they make no distinction of sex in their appointment of commanders).[33] Although no other names of reigning queens are known beyond those of the celebrated duo, Cartimandua and Boudica, these constitute one-third of the total of all the known names of sovereigns/chieftains. When King Prasutagus of the Iceni died in about AD 60, there was an established client-queen presiding over the vast Brigantian territories, a client-queen already supported once by the Romans in difficult circumstances. On grounds of gender alone, Prasutagus had no reason to suppose that his wife Boudica would be unacceptable to the Romans as regent of the kingdom after his death.

With the death of King Prasutagus, the pace of Boudica's story quickens; at the same time the areas where speculation must substitute for certainty by no means diminish. Sir Ronald Syme once wisely observed that conjecture cannot be avoided: 'otherwise history is not writing, for it does not become intelligible'.[34] This is undoubtedly a comforting maxim for the student of Boudica.

Speculation as opposed to certainty gets off to a spanking start in view of the fact that there are only three written sources for the Boudican rebellion which have any claim to be regarded as primary; and one of these survives in an edited form made nine hundred years later. Two of these sources come from the pen of Tacitus, who touched upon the Boudican rebellion both in his *Agricola*, the life of his father-in-law published in about AD 98, and in his *Annals* written fifteen to twenty years later. The third comes from Dio Cassius, who was born in Nicaea, where his father was a senator, in about 163; a monk called Xiphilinus of Trapezus produced 'epitomes' of his work, selections for public reading which included his passage about Boudica, in the second half of the eleventh century.[35]

None of these three accounts is very long. And at first sight each of the three claims to be regarded as a primary source may seem rather tenuous in view of the fact that Dio was born a hundred years after the revolt and even Tacitus a mere five years before it. Fortunately Tacitus, quite apart from his diligent researches in the imperial archives, was able to benefit from the first-hand testimony of his father-in-law. For Agricola as a young man was present in Britain, a member of the Governor's staff, at the time of these stirring events; whatever old men forget, they do not forget the campaigns of their youth. There were other survivors he might have interviewed: the widow of Ostorius Scapula lived on for many years, Tacitus being consul in the same year as his grandson. He has also increased his store of knowledge between writing the *Agricola* and the *Annals*.[36]

Dio's claim is based more modestly on the fact that although there are traces of his having read Tacitus' account, he does not simply reproduce it. On the contrary, so far as can be judged from Xiphilinus' selection, Dio had access to other independent material which has since vanished. It is known that he spent ten years taking notes on the work of other historians.[37]

Mercifully, this paucity of written sources concerning the Boudican episode is counteracted by the burgeoning discoveries of archaeology. Since the Second World War new methods of

ploughing and above all the development of aerial reconnais-
sance in course of such pastoral duties as crop-spraying have led
to fresh and exciting finds, even if the increasing demands of
the American NATO bases upon East Anglian airspace are
beginning to act restrictively.[38] Nevertheless, the fact that the
actual date of the rebellion remains the subject of controversy –
with dedicated proponents of both AD 60 and 61 – does
illustrate the undeniable problems caused by this dearth of
evidence.

The argument arises over Tacitus' own placing of the rebellion
in 61, a date which does not fit with other information he supplies
concerning the governors in Britain and the consulates in Rome.
His narrative however makes sense, if the rebellion is put back to
60; the other events such as the change of governors then follow
naturally. As against that, Tacitus' care as an historian casts doubt
on such a mistake in dating. It is not however a controversy
which is of vital interest to the present study of Boudica. Since
the preponderance of historians still appear to favour 60, despite
some strong contenders in the 61 party, this is the date which
without prejudice will here be adopted.[39]

At least the fact of King Prasutagus' death is incontrovertible.
What else is certain? He died in 60 – or maybe 59 – having been
longa opulentia clarus – long renowned for his wealth. He died as a
client-king of the Roman Empire, a position which, at least from
the point of view of the Romans, made his dominions an integral
part of that empire – *membra partesque*. He died, we must assume,
without male heirs, since the will he made did not mention them,
and did mention two daughters. He did not leave the kingdom to
his wife, Boudica, but he did entrust her with the regency on
behalf of these girls.[40]

The clause in Prasutagus' will which was however to stir up the
most trouble at the time, and prove the undoing of his family
thereafter, was not to do with the regency. It was to do with that
wealth for which he had long been renowned. Prasutagus left
his lands and personal possessions partly to the Emperor, and
partly to his wife in trust for his daughters (although the exact

proportions of the inheritance due to each are not known).[41] He must have hoped that by so doing he had provided for a peaceful hand-over. It was an idle hope.

CHAPTER FIVE

Ruin by a Woman

Moreover, all this ruin was brought upon the Romans
by a woman, a fact which in itself caused them the
greatest shame.

DIO CASSIUS

Boudica, the widow in whom King Prasutagus of the Iceni
had placed such trust, was of royal birth. This much we
know from the *Agricola*. But Tacitus, with his eponymous
taciturnity, actually leaves open the question of whether she
belonged to the royal family of the Iceni or another one. He
simply says that Boudica was *generis regii femina*, a phrase that can
be (and has been) variously translated as 'a woman of the Royal
house' and 'a lady of royal descent'. The Greek of Dio Cassius
reads less equivocally: 'A Briton woman of the royal family.'[1]

It is theoretically possible, therefore, that Boudica was actually
a princess from a neighbouring tribe. It would be romantically
fitting, for example, to derive Boudica from the Brigantes, where
that strong female leadership was being exercised from the 40s
onwards. Making Boudica the sister, daughter or niece of
Cartimandua has, however, no evidence to support it, beyond
the vaguely comforting feeling that the only two known Warrior
Queens of the period must have been related to each other. (But
this is to treat a Warrior Queen as a rarity: as has been pointed out
in Chapter Four, this was not necessarily so.) Nor is there any
proper evidence for the equally pleasing tradition which has
Boudica hailing from Ireland. (The known existence of Irish
queens in later centuries and the similarity of the Norfolk torcs to
those found in Ireland does not seem quite enough.)[2] In the
absence of such evidence, it seems far more likely that, as Tacitus

implies and Dio Cassius states, the royal house to which Boudica belonged was that of the Iceni: the tribe she would now successfully stir to action.

Neither Dio nor Tacitus helps us with Boudica's exact age at the time of the rebellion. It is a fair guess that she was somewhere in her thirties. In 60 we know that Boudica had two living daughters who had reached the age of puberty, who were not married and who needed their mother's regency. If these daughters were in their teens, and thus born some time around 45 or 46, a rough calculation brings Boudica's birth to AD 26 or 27, and at least AD 30. It is this calculation, incidentally, which makes it virtually certain that she was married to Prasutagus at the time of the first rebellion of the Iceni in 49, a mere eleven years previously; otherwise this was a remarkably short period in which to cram marriage and the birth of two children who had reached a nubile age. But if Boudica is not likely to have been under thirty in 60, she could of course have been quite a bit older; supposing these daughters were merely the youngest survivors of a large family, Boudica could have been forty or more. Her precise age, like so much else about her, remains guesswork.

Dio, unlike Tacitus, does give a physical description of the British Queen. She had red hair – a mass of 'the tawniest hair' hanging to her waist – and she was very tall, 'in appearance almost terrifying', with a fierce expression. These attributes were not unusual for her sex and race, at least according to the Classical writers. The proverbial Celtic colouring has been mentioned. The size and indeed strength of Celtic women was also something on which they were prone to comment: Diodorus Siculus went further and complimented them on being the equals of their husbands in courage as well. A celebrated anecdote of Ammianus Marcellinus has a Gaul's wife, even stronger than her husband, battling with swelled-out neck and grinding teeth, flailing her arms like a windmill, and delivering kicks at the same time 'like missiles from a catapult'.[3]

Boudica also had a notably harsh voice, according to Dio. This is a comment which has an additional interest in a study of the

Warrior Queen at various periods, since again and again the question of the voice will arise. Condemnation of a female leader very often throws in the fact that her voice is harsh or strident. In 1400 Leonardo Bruno instructed Battista Malatesta that 'if a woman throws her arms around whilst speaking, or if she increases the volume of her speech with greater forcefulness, she will appear threateningly insane and requiring restraint. These matters belong to men, as war, or battles . . .' As will be seen, allusions to Mrs Thatcher's 'fishwife' voice have been frequent in the 1980s.[4]

At the same time approval for a given Warrior Queen frequently takes the form of endowing her with a persistently dulcet tone, in spite of circumstances when any voice, male or female, might be pardoned for being raised. Thus Matilda of Tuscany, although both tall and strong, retained 'a wonderfully sweet voice', in the account of an admiring monastic chronicler. The Rani of Jhansi, on the other hand, who led the Indian sepoys following the mutiny of 1857, was allowed a remarkably fine figure by the British, but 'what spoilt her was her voice'. The best kind of voice for a female leader, achieved by few, was that allowed to the third-century Queen Zenobia of Palmyra by a contemporary commentator: *vox clara et virilis* – 'clear and like that of a man' (which Gibbon, however, translated as 'strong and harmonious' – in the eighteenth century, women were not allowed to have manly voices).[5]

Maybe, then, Dio Cassius, who was not after all present to hear Boudica haranguing the Iceni, endowed her with her harsh voice because it was in keeping with what might be expected of a Celtic Warrior Queen; maybe his informants made the same assumption for him. It is even possible that Dio knew nothing of her appearance and merely granted Boudica the likely attributes of such a person. Leaving aside these imponderables, it is sufficient to state that it is from this, Dio's short but vivid account of the strapping, red-haired Warrior Queen, that all other descriptions of her, to say nothing of later impersonations, have flowed.

Dr Johnson once described this world as one in which 'much

is to be done and little to be known'. That certainly stands for the narrower world of Boudican research. But the nebulous nature of the information available about Queen Boudica should not cause too much dismay; at least, not in terms of the period in which she lived. It has been pointed out that in a revolt which involved perhaps as many as one hundred thousand people, only ten names are known, all from Tacitus.[6] (Dio added none.) Two are British – Prasutagus and Boudica – and the rest Roman. One more name, that of a Roman woman, Julia Pacata, emerged when the tombstone she commissioned for her husband, Julius Classicianus, was discovered.

It is the contrast between this nebulosity, characteristic of the first century AD and Boudica's – or rather Boadicea's – subsequent transcendent fame, which makes the lack of information so tantalizing. (Although it has to be admitted, from the point of view of myth rather than history, that the fire of popular interest often burns all the more brightly for the lack of dampening facts to pour upon it: Boadicea's lively leaping myth being no doubt a case in point.)

The local Roman administration reacted immediately and unfavourably to the will of King Prasutagus. The latter's intention in dividing his estate and treasure was presumably to placate the Emperor and safeguard his family's inheritance at one and the same time. In the event Prasutagus succeeded in doing neither. But this is not to say that the expedient of sacrificing part of the inheritance in order to ensure the safe bestowal of the rest was a wild or even an original plan. Not only did the Roman nobility of this period often resort to the same device to protect the terms of their wills, but the range and number of royal wills involving Rome has recently been shown to be far greater than is sometimes supposed.[7]

Unfortunately in this case the officials on the spot were either unsympathetic or rapacious – or both. They ignored the will of the King. Representatives of the Procurator Catus Decianus – the chief financial administrator of the British province – seized all the King's estate and the total of his treasure. That was not the end of the depredations. Not only did the Iceni nobles find their own hereditary estates treated as though forfeit to the Romans – for no crime except the death of their king – but members of Prasutagus' own court were humiliated and maltreated. It is obvious that the Iceni nobility, a free-born and independent caste, suffered an extraordinary and unwelcome change in their status. In Tacitus' menacing words: 'Kingdom and household alike were plundered like prizes of war.'[8]

The first step taken by the Procurator's representatives was however in a different class so far as sheer inhumanity and public insult was concerned. Brutally, Boudica, the new Queen of the Iceni, was flogged. Her two daughters, those princesses designated as heiresses by their dead father, were raped.

The names of these young girls, like so many other women's names throughout history, are unknown. Rape, equally, is a fate which has been shared by countless women down the ages, both named and nameless; victims of a male aggression, at once casual and horrifying, simply because, historically speaking, they happened to find themselves in the wrong place at the wrong time. That Roman conquest was not altogether free from this can be seen from the speech made by the Caledonian Calgacus, facing Agricola in battle some twenty years after the Boudican revolt, and reported to Tacitus. He urged on his men by castigating the enemy: 'They rob, kill and rape and this they call Roman rule.' In this case however it is impossible to regard the violation of Boudica's daughters as in any way mindless. This was a deliberate act of policy and as such it was symbolic: this act of rape was what Susan Brownmiller has called 'the vehicle of *his* victorious conquest over *her* being': he in this case being a Roman and she an Iceni royal princess.[9]

Symbolic too was the flogging of the Queen: or scourging, to be exact, for Tacitus' words are *verberis adfecta* – literally, to put to the rods. In principle, the Romans were not merciless or brutal to their captive royal women. One would not expect Cleopatra to have suffered such a fate, nor did she herself anticipate it: for the proud spirit of the 'Queen of War' the prospect of exhibition in a Roman triumph was humiliation enough. The wife and daughter of the British Caratacus were shown clemency once they had performed their own part in Claudius' triumph. On the other hand, the rape of the royal female as a ritual act to signify the suppression of a people is one with obvious psychological connotations.

The young Cesare Borgia held Caterina Sforza, then in her late thirties, incommunicado for a period after he had finally succeeded in storming her stronghold of Ravaldino in 1499; he then committed 'injustices' to her body. This was not lust, nor was she acquiescent (despite Cesare Borgia's coarse joke to his officers afterwards that Caterina had defended her fortress better than her virtue).[10] Cesare Borgia's act of rape was intended to signify the collapse of Caterina Sforza's spirited political and military campaign for independence.

It is generally assumed by historians that some act of defiance on the part of the Iceni must have preceded this brutality of the Romans towards their royal women.[11] Certainly this is perfectly possible, given the natural temperament for resistance the Iceni had displayed in 49 and would shortly display again. But as a matter of fact Tacitus does not say so. On the contrary he lists the cruelties of the Romans (starting with the flogging of Boudica and the rape of her daughters) and then moves to the consequences: 'These outrages and the fear of worse . . . moved the Iceni to arms.' So perhaps an unconscious assumption has been made by these historians, in view of the bestiality of the Romans' behaviour, that some gesture or gestures of dissent *must* have taken place to provoke it.

Tacitus, writing shortly after the event, shows proper understanding of the way subject peoples are frequently handled. Given his order of events, the Romans' pitiless treatment of Boudica and her daughters was intended not so much to punish the Iceni for defiance but to emphasize their subordinate status and the uselessness of resistance to Roman rule. The fact that the royal family of the Iceni contained, coincidentally, two young females gave the Romans a nice opportunity for that extra-symbolic violence of rape. As for the scourging administered to the Iceni Queen, the Romans happened to believe that women as a whole were incapable of rule because they were incapable of discipline: 'Woman is a violent and uncontrolled animal, and it is no good giving her the reins and expecting her not to kick over the traces': these were the supposed words of Cato the elder in 195 BC, as reported by Livy two hundred years later on the eve of the Boudican period.[12] To be able to 'control' a woman and figuratively control the Iceni at the same time was another fitting coincidence.

If it was just this symbolic Roman brutality which touched off the Iceni revolt, demonstrating that a Warrior Queen can personify her people to the oppressed as well as the oppressor, that was not its sole cause. For such an intense conflagration as now threatened to destroy the whole basis of the Roman occupation could hardly be set off by that brutality alone, however shocking. It was Boudica who led her people in the general uprising, Tacitus noting at this point that lack of distinction between the sexes in the Britons' appointment of commanders referred to earlier. Furthermore Tacitus had Boudica allude to the outrages performed upon her own body and those of her daughters in the speech he put into her mouth to encourage her warriors on the eve of battle. Nevertheless the rebellion itself had deeper underlying causes. The mere fact that the other tribes to whom Boudica's wrongs would be less personally shocking joined in with the Iceni under Boudica's leadership, shows that this was in fact a widespread as well as dangerous protest against the excesses of Roman rule.

Financial exploitation and land appropriation, two slow-burning fuses liable finally to cause an explosion in any society, were at the centre of the problem. According to Dio, the rebels found 'an excuse for the war' in the fact that certain sums of money granted to leading Britons by the Emperor Claudius and believed to have been gifts were now declared to be mere loans. The Procurator, Catus Decianus, he who was also responsible for the confiscation of that part of Prasutagus' estate willed to his daughters, proceeded to demand the return of these 'loans'. At the same time, Dio accused Seneca, the celebrated Roman philosopher and politician, of first imposing an unwanted financial loan upon the Britons (attracted by the good rate of interest) and then suddenly recalling it in a series of severe measures.[13]

Whatever the truth of these particular exactions – perhaps Dio's cases merely serve to illustrate the general Roman use of short-sighed exploitive methods – the picture which emerges of the Roman administration of its new province is not a pretty one. The Romans were certainly not pursuing that policy of concili-ation towards and co-operation with the local magnates most likely to ensure the long-term pacification of 'Roman' Britain. The tribal men of property began by resenting this treatment and ended by rising up against it, since they no longer had anything to gain by backing the Roman cause.[14]

The case of the Roman temple at Camulodunum (Colchester) exemplifies this process of exploitation. The situation in and around Camulodunum was already disturbing for the native Trinovantes in view of the arrogance with which the Roman occupation was carried out. The Roman town of Camulodunum had been founded about twelve years previously. It was designed not as a military stronghold, but as a *colonia*, that is to say, a settlement of Roman army veterans who had received grants of land in the surrounding *territorium* administered by the town, in place of gratuities at the end of their period of service. The term *colonia* also meant that an existing town or city was accorded special municipal status. (Camulodunum was in fact the first town in Britain to receive it.)

The establishment of a *colonia* was always a matter of explicit imperial policy and it was a direct decree from the Emperor Claudius which had brought into being Roman Camulodunum. The intention, obviously, was the 'Romanization' of the new province; civilizing loyal veterans would gradually spread and multiply among the rude British.[15] The native Trinovantes, of course did not see it quite like that; in particular their reactions were not helped by the manner in which the ex-soldiers possessed themselves of their grants. According to Tacitus, 'the settlers drove the Trinovantes from their homes and land, and called them prisoners and slaves'. Furthermore, excavations at Colchester have revealed the cruel conditions in which the native workers were kept, as they were obliged to carry out the construction works of their conquerors.[16] When the ex-soldiers helped themselves to more land than was legally granted, their comrades still in arms turned a blind eye, hoping for the same licence themselves. With all this in mind, it is not difficult to see how the oppressed Trinovantes, whether the tribal aristocrats or their humbler followers, might brood upon their wrongs.

The temple, erected to the Emperor Claudius at Camulodunum, may have been intended by the Romans to imbue the native Trinovantes with loyalty to their new masters, but that was very far from being the effect it had upon them. On the contrary, the temple appeared, according to Tacitus, as the 'blatant stronghold of alien rule'. The whole concept of civic monument was alien to Celtic society. Moreover the sylvan temples of the Celtic religion had a very different air. This edifice proposing the godhead of a foreign emperor had nothing sublime about it to the indignant eyes of the Trinovantes. What was more, they were expected to pay for it.

It is not clear exactly how much of the temple of Claudius had already been erected by AD 60, since it is no longer thought that construction was begun during the Emperor's lifetime.[17] It would therefore have been building costs, rather than the maintenance of a priesthood to service the temple, which fell upon the Trinovantes. A series of discoveries, beginning in the late seventeenth century when the existing Norman castle (erected in the eleventh century) was demolished, have, however, given some idea of how the hated temple must have looked.

In 1683 the contractor found vaults below the Norman floor; in 1919 Sir Mortimer Wheeler and P. G. Laver revealed that the castle actually enclosed the *podium* or platform of the temple;

further excavations have followed in 1950 (the 1,900th anniversary of the foundation of the *colonia*) and 1964. Calculations made from the surviving walls and piers suggest that the temple itself measured some 150 feet by 80 feet, that it was surrounded by a colonnade of columns, thirty-five feet high and over three feet in diameter, and fronted by a sweeping flight of steps where there would have been a series of statues.[*][18] Enough of this was already completed to provide a clear and imposing focus for the resentful eye: enough, as it turned out, was already completed to provide a target for destruction.

According to Tacitus, the town of Camulodunum gave out its own desperate but unheeded warning of what lay ahead. The portents were many and various. The statue of Victory fell down with its back turned as though it was fleeing the enemy. Outlandish yells were heard in the senate-house and shrieks in the local theatre (the Romans had indeed gone for those amenities which made their civilization so agreeable to them while ignoring the prime need of maintaining walls round the town). A phantom settlement in ruins was glimpsed at the head of the River Thames. Most troubling of all was the blood-red colour of the sea, and the shapes like human corpses found abandoned at the edge of the shore by the ebb-tide.

Gazing on all these things, the native Britons began to hope – and the Roman settlers began to tremble.

Elsewhere in Britain, there were other frenzied women to be found. These women were not merely chanting, they were delivering their chants as war-cries against the Romans. For as the Iceni rose in revolt, led by the outraged Queen, and the subjugated Trinovantes planned to join them, the Governor of Britain, Suetonius Paulinus, was on the faraway island of Mona

---

[*] A reconstruction at the Castle Museum, Colchester, shows a building of gleaming white, with ostentatious red, blue and golden ornamentation; Roman eagles and a triumphant statue of the Emperor Claudius at the front steps make it easy to understand Tacitus' reference to a blatant stronghold.

(Anglesey). Here, in the celebrated sanctuary of the Druids, numbers of rebels against Roman rule had taken refuge. Suetonius' mission was one of search and destroy. Moreover the destruction was intended to encompass not only the rebels, but also the host of Druids as well.

The scene at Mona is vividly described by Tacitus. The dense armed mass of the enemy confronting the Roman army included 'black-robed women with dishevelled hair like Furies, brandishing torches'. Close by stood the Druids, 'raising their hands to heaven and screaming dreadful curses'. For an instant the Roman host stood as if paralysed by the weird spectacle. But then they urged each other, and were indeed urged by Suetonius himself, not to be afraid of a pack of fanatical women.

In that businesslike way which had made their soldiers the disciplined wonder of the world, the Romans bore irresistibly down on the varied multitudes of their opponents. Curses and women's cries were no match for them. The torches of these Celtic Furies were actually turned against their brandishers. After the assault, in an equally businesslike fashion, Suetonius had the sacred groves of Mona cut down, so that, as Tacitus put it, Mona's 'barbarous superstitions' could no longer be practised; in these Tacitus included the drenching of the altars in the blood of prisoners, and the consulting of the gods by human entrails. From Suetonius' point of view it had been a highly satisfactory operation. In that military rivalry with Corbulo to which Tacitus attests, he had now surely scored a victory to rank with Corbulo's conquest of Armenia.

It was at that very moment that the news of the horrifying disaster which had overcome the Roman settlers of the eastern *colonia* reached him.

Suetonius was by now a man of about sixty. As a veteran commander, he knew how to handle the kind of mountain warfare with which the Welsh terrain confronted him: he had campaigned in the High Atlas mountains.[19] He had been Governor of Mauretania, and in a distinguished career had shown himself not only a brilliant general but also an accomplished politician. The question remains as to why, at this combustible moment in the history of the province he had been ruling for the last two years, he found himself at the very limits of his territory: as far from the turbulences in the east as it was possible to be.

Was it a coincidence? Was Suetonius merely led on by his own military ambitions at what proved to be an exceptionally ill-timed moment? Or is there some more sinister – and more exciting – interpretation to be placed upon the fact that Suetonius was besieging the Druid sanctuary at the exact moment that the eastern tribes chose to rebel?

As the priest-class of Celtic society, the Druids were drawn from among the tribal aristocracy.[20] The Druids of Gaul in the time of Caesar at least, were believed to constitute an important nationalist focus for their people. Caesar was also convinced – a hundred years before the Boudican revolt – that Druidism was an import from Britain to Gaul, with Druids returning to Britain again in order to refresh their knowledge. Even if the Druids were not as politically influential as was supposed by the Romans, it was this belief which was the important point. At any rate, the Druids were suppressed, either for their 'barbarous practices' (the official reason given) or for their political activities.[21]

What were these barbarous practices? The normal priestly concerns of the Druids were all those of ritual magic, including of course intercession to the gods via animal sacrifice. Gibbon acquitted the Druids of actual *human* sacrifice, supposing the charge to be a mere excuse for suppressing them on other (political) grounds, and wrote feelingly of the Celtic religion: 'the deities of a thousand groves and a thousand streams possessed in peace their local and respective influence'.[22] But it is generally believed nowadays that the references are too numerous to be ignored; at some point in the past the Druids must have practised it, though it may well have died out by the first century BC.[23]

Human sacrifice was something from which the Romans shrank in fastidious horror (although the unarmed Christians, matched in the arena against wild beasts for the delectation of the emperor and the Roman crowd, might have found such disgust ironical). The notion of human sacrifice, like the notion of nationalist political influence, combined conveniently to present the image of a body both hateful and threatening and thus ripe for suppression. This is not to dismiss Gibbon's equally evocative image of tranquil sylvan deities, which may represent another part of the truth.

In the early nineteenth century Gérard de Nerval wrote of the history of the death of religions as being even more terrifying than the history of the fall of great empires: 'all of us must sometimes tremble to find so many dark gates opening out to nothingness'.[24] Certainly to contemplate the Druids themselves in the absence of any literature (non-existent because they were non-literate) is to gaze through a very dark gate indeed. The Classical writers, who must under the circumstances remain our only guides, are not necessarily equipped for the task. To discern actual policy in the disparate actions of a body, whose motives and practices are completely alien, is difficult if not impossible.

Returning to the British Druids of Mona, a hundred years after the time of Caesar, they were, according to Tacitus, harbouring rebels at their sanctuary, thus transforming it into a form of political refuge. Does that mean that Druids of first-century Britain were also busily fomenting anti-Roman feelings elsewhere?[25] In short, were the British Druids actually responsible for the coincidence – the planned coincidence – of the East Anglian uprising and Suetonius' absence in remotest Wales? Tempting as such a theory might be, there is no hard evidence for such a collusion. That might not be relevant if, as was suggested by Sir Cyril Fox, the Druidic hierarchy were busy organizing the gold trade of the Iceni via the sea ports of the Wash.[26] Certainly the coastal access of the Iceni, which made their peaceful attitudes interesting to the Romans, is not to be ignored.

In the absence of any proof, however, one is thrown back on the palpable injustices which the Iceni had unquestionably endured, as had the Trinovantes to the south. There was quite enough here to whip up a revolt. It therefore seems more plausible to regard the uprising now led by Boudica as a spontaneous explosion for which there were deep-rooted causes, financial and economic, with a particular incitement of the Iceni arising from the treatment of their queen, rather than something planned or fomented by the Druids of Mona.

If there was a religious dimension to the Boudican revolt – and it seems from Dio's account of the British behaviour that there was – then it sprang from two sources. One was that natural equation of a popular religion and political resistance which occurs when the religion of the conqueror is markedly different from that of the conquered. (Irish history since 1650, the Catholicism of the people versus the Protestantism of the Ascendancy, is the classic example of this.) Such an equation needed no encouragement from afar. The second source would be Boudica's own self-identification as a religious figure, whether as priestess, prophetess or even quasi-goddess.

Boudica, according to Dio, addressed her tribe at enormous length on the eve of the rout which would lead them towards Camulodunum. The enunciation of such elaborate orations, if not the common practice of barbarian Warrior Queens (we cannot know), was certainly the common practice of Classical historians, who were accustomed to put these setpieces into the mouths of their characters on appropriately dire, solemn or patriotic occasions. Tacitus gives Boudica his version of a speech both queenly and bellicose at a later point: on the eve of the final battle.

Dio begins his account with that physical description of Boudica quoted earlier, gives her a spear to rattle in her fist ('to shew herself the more dreadful', as Holinshed would later have it) and describes her clothing: 'a tunic of diverse colours over which a thick mantle was fastened with a brooch'. This, he tells us, was her invariable attire. He then elevates her high on a tribunal, the kind of raised platform used by Roman magistrates and generals. The speech which follows has not fared well at the hands of later historians. Milton, in fine misogynist form, sneered at it in his

History of Britain. He ran it together with Tacitus' version and put Boudica, somewhat opprobriously, 'on a high heap of Turves in a loose-bodied gown [so much for her Celtic dress] declaiming . . . fondly', that is, foolishly. 'A deal of other fondness they [Dio and Tacitus] put into her mouth, not worth recital; how she was lash'd, how her Daughters were hand'd, things worthier silence, retirement, and a Veil, than for a Woman to repeat as done to her own person, or to hear repeated before an host of men.' Sir Ronald Syme, who otherwise found Dio's account 'verbose and miserable', regarded the speech as 'a monstrosity'; more recently it has been described as 'long, not to say exhaustive'.[27]

Clearly Boudica did not address her tribe in the terms given to us by a second-century Greek, epitomized by an eleventh-century monk and here translated into early-twentieth-century English. But the sentiments she is made to express do at least serve to remind one quite vividly of the recent treatment of the Britons at the hands of the Romans. Boudica talks about the difference between freedom and slavery which they have learned from experience (Tacitus at this point merely has the Britons in general, without mention of Boudica, arguing for freedom over slavery) and touches on their ancestral mode of life, boasting of their hardiness. She points out how the Britons have suffered since the Romans appeared in Britain. 'Have we not been robbed entirely of most of our possessions, and those the greatest, while for those that remain we pay taxes?' Although the Britons should rightly have repelled the Romans when they first invaded, it is not too late for them to act now, if only for the sake of their children, lest they too be raised up in bondage.

It is however what Boudica does, rather than what she says, which gives its importance to Dio's account. For having spoken, the Queen suddenly released a hare from the folds of her dress 'as a species of divination'. As the hare fled, it was seen by the multitude to run 'in the auspicious direction'. There were general shouts of delight at what was clearly a favourable omen for the uprising (as it was clearly intended to be, for one imagines that Boudica, astute enough to install the hare, was also astute enough to ensure that it ran in the right direction). The choice of a hare was also deliberate. This is an animal which features mysteriously and excitingly in the mythology of many countries, from the Far East to the pre-conquest inhabitants of North America, and it had been mentioned already by Caesar as among those animals sacred to the Britons. Various traces of hares in outline and other depictions of them as hunted beasts have been preserved; these may well have religious significance.[28]

Boudica then prayed to a goddess named Andraste (or Andaste in one manuscript). 'I thank thee, Andraste, and call upon thee as woman speaking to woman.' Although this is the only specific mention of the name Andraste/Andaste, it may well relate, given the process of translation and epitomization, to that of the goddess of the Vocontii in south-east Gaul, Andarta, and a general British goddess of Victory, mentioned by Dio later, Andate. It could also be some compound derived from Anu, one of the names of the Celtic super-goddess, the mother of all the mothers, as it were. The name is however less important than the type: for while the local Celtic deities have hundreds of names, the types remain consistent. Andraste was presumably the war-goddess of the Iceni. (One goddess portrayed on an Iceni coin 'with an individuality and a vigour atypical of classical art' may be intended to depict Andraste.)[29]

This is not the unique reference to a woman enacting a prophetic role in this period. Tacitus commented that the German tribe 'traditionally regard many of the female sex as prophetic, and indeed, by excess of superstition, as divine'. About ten years after the Boudican uprising, 'an unmarried woman' designated as Veleda (the word in Celtic implies the functions of a prophetess) was described by him as enjoying wide influence over some Rhinelanders called the Bructeri.[30] A captured legionary legate, Munius Lupercus, was despatched to her as a gift, although put to death before she could bend him to her purposes, whatever they might have been. Veleda's prestige was further enhanced when she foretold the massacre of the Roman army at Vetera. Later Veleda was used as an intermediary by the citizens of Cologne. Personal approaches to Veleda, of any sort, were not permitted; her relatives, with the idea of increasing the aura of veneration about her, kept her immured in a high tower, one of their number transmitting questions and answers, 'as if he were mediating between a god and his worshippers'. Nor did the Romans attempt to dispute her sacred credentials: it seems that when they finally captured Veleda, she was installed in the service of a temple at Ardea.[31]

Similarly Boudica – whose eventual fate was to be very different – in releasing her hare and issuing her supplication not only associated herself with the goddess, but assumed a composite role of priestess, prophetess and war leader – Holy (Armed) Figurehead – in accordance with Celtic tradition and myth.

So Boudica, Queen and leader of the Iceni, swept down upon hapless Camulodunum in her chariot. She had assembled an initial host of 120,000 according to Dio. It was the apparent suddenness of the attack upon a defenceless city which made it so horrifying in its consequences. But of course the fact of a British assault should not have come upon the Roman inhabitants so suddenly, just as Camulodunum itself should not have been so defenceless. The suddenness was not so much in the British attack itself, as in the minds of the Romans who faced it.

The Roman veterans, happily enjoying their generous grants of land, including those tracts to which they had helped themselves, must have ignored other signs, which should have been more telling to them than the blood-red sea and the outlandish cries in the theatre. Tacitus mentions the fifth column within the city who made sure that it was not defended properly; but this fifth column (*occulti rebellionis conscii*, literally 'secret conspirators in the rebellion') must have consisted of native Trinovantes, whose loyalties, given that they were first dispossessed, then ill-treated, should never have been taken for granted.

To explain the Roman negligence, Donald R. Dudley and Graham Webster, authors of the authoritative study *The Rebellion of Boudicca*, called attention to 'that overconfidence that often besets colonial powers'. Writing in 1962, they pointed out that the British had shown an equally negligent attitude towards the Mau Mau tribal insurrection in its first stages, for which oversight an official report had recently criticized the government of Kenya.[32] The comparison is certainly a valid one, not only for the tribal– nationalist character of both uprisings. The Roman settlers of Camulodunum, confronted by a series of atrocities apparently totally unheralded, must have experienced something like the same appalled bewilderment as the British settlers of Kenya some nineteen hundred years later.

The plain fact was that the Romans simply could not conceive that the Britons could do this to them: rise up, sack a city and massacre its inhabitants. History after all provides plenty of examples of this kind of tragic error. It is a common mistake on the part of the conquering power to consider a rebellion of the conquered to be impossible, because they find it unbelievable. The Romans of Camulodunum merely joined in this error and suffered for it.

Nor was disbelief confined to Camulodunum itself. Once the situation was accepted within the *colonia* for what it was – serious but not yet desperate – there was still time for the veteran settlers to send for reinforcements from London to the few men still under arms at Camulodunum. Here, however, the Procurator Catus Decianus, showing himself to be complacent as well as rapacious, thought it sufficient to despatch a mere two hundred men (who would perish with their former comrades). Around the wall-less town itself not even a rampart or a palisade was erected, for which there must have been time if reinforcements could still be summoned from afar.[33] Most tragic of all, the women, the children and the old people were not sent away.

The town was overrun without difficulty. Archaeological evidence not only confirms that there were no walls – as Tacitus stated – but that the original defences erected by the legionaries had actually been levelled down. Over them were built a series of houses made of wattle-and-stake, and filled in and covered with daub. These houses were separated by narrow gravelled alleys. All of this would be easy to destroy by fire – and it was. So fierce was the fire that whole buildings became baked into a kind of clay: a section of one such house (discovered in 1972 in the Lion Walk near the site of the temple) can still be seen preserved in the Colchester Castle Museum. The carbonized remains of twill mattresses were found, and other domestic objects such as Samian ware, burned black, as well as food: the charred remains of imported fruits, including dates, plums and figs.[34]

Even today, in modern Colchester, traces can be seen of a way of life which came to a halt abruptly nearly two thousand years ago. (Modern Colchester has incidentally considerable archaeological value as a site since it had to be totally rebuilt by the Romans following the holocaust of AD 60, allowing precise dating for certain discoveries.) The excavated site of a centurion's camp gives the visitor a strange Pompeian feeling of the past arrested. This camp, founded about twelve years before, would have been part of the sketchy defences of the town. A Roman grid cooking-iron has been discovered (such grids, by being pressed flat into the earth, have a good chance of survival). One may reflect that the last meal cooked on that iron was cooked in AD 60.[35]

Moreover there have been plenty of new opportunities for excavation, due to the levelling of one lot of buildings and the erection of another as the town has been rebuilt by stages during the twentieth century. In that brief interval allowed by the grace of the developer can be seen once again the blackened Samian ware and the scorched earth – literally – of the Boudican sack: an extraordinary orange-red hue.[*] However, curiously enough, of actual skeletons there are very few traces. It is to be assumed that sometime later the Romans came back and cremated the remains of their slaughtered comrades.

Three surviving artefacts, two of them of stone and one of

---

[*] As for example at a site in Culver Street, Colchester, destined eventually to be a car park, visited by the author in the summer of 1985 when it was worked by the Colchester Archaeological Unit.

bronze, also bear witness to the savagery of the British attack – as also to the motives which inspired it. At some point the British tribes swooped down upon the Roman cemetery to the west of the town where the old soldiers had been interred, as it was hoped, for an eternal rest after their long and honourable labours. The tombstone of one Marcus Favonius Facilis of the XXth Legion shows him standing confidently in full military panoply, including his *vituus* or vinestick (the modern swagger stick) in his right hand and his sword in his left. But the tombstone (discovered in 1868) has been broken into two pieces; more significantly still, the face has been hacked away.

In 1928 another tombstone was discovered, that of a man who died at the age of forty belonging to the first *Ala* (auxiliary cavalry unit) of the Thracians. Named as Longinus Sdapezematygus, his adoption of a Roman name in addition to his Thracian one was a characteristic practice. Unfortunately for his survival, Longinus was depicted as mounted upon an enormous rampant horse while below him crouched some troglodyte figure of a man, who probably symbolized death, but could well have had to the British attackers a more unpleasant symbolism of subjugation. At all events the tombstone of Longinus Sdapezematygus has been set about with a will, the face of Longinus himself and the nose of his horse violently obliterated.

Lastly, a bronze head of the Emperor Claudius was fished out of the River Alde, near Saxmundham in Suffolk, in 1907 by an astonished boy who had gone swimming. This head too has been subjected to violet treatment, as can be seen from the jagged edges at the neck where it has been hacked away from the body. Once thought to be the head of the great equestrian statue of the Emperor which would have fronted the temple erected to his memory, its comparatively moderate size and provincial technique are now considered to rule out that possibility. It must have belonged to some lesser statue erected in the body of the town. From the point of view of the sack of Camulodunum, it is of course more evocative to regard this head as one which might have been once carried on a pole through the burning streets of the *colonia* – if not the live head of the Emperor, at least the symbolic head of the enemy.[*] Since the Alde findspot is in Iceni territory, one imagines that the head, a peculiarly incriminating piece of evidence, was finally flung away there, after the defeat of the tribe.[36]

The temple itself held out for two more days following the sack of the town. The old soldiers congregated there as in a redoubt for one last desperate effort to survive until reinforcements came. Weapons and armour, rusty with disuse, have been discovered, which the veterans must have hastily routed out and donned.[37] The picture of these old warhorses, once the masters of Europe, now destined to die, antiquated weapons to hand, at the hands of the despised barbarians outside the limits of the known world (as they had once complained to Claudius) has its own poignancy. For unlike Lucknow and Mafeking, there was to be no relief for this particular garrison. The gaudy temple was battered down and fired, the veterans, like their families, put to the sword.

The Britons under Boudica surveyed the smoking town and turned their faces towards London. For the Romans, when news of the holocaust reached them, there was an additional humiliation to be faced. 'Moreover,' wrote Dio Cassius, 'all this ruin was brought upon [them] by a woman, a fact which in itself caused them the greatest shame.'

[*] It is now in the British Museum. Both the military tombstones can be seen in the Castle Museum, Colchester.

CHAPTER SIX

The Red Layer

~~~

Far below the modern streets of the City of London the
events of AD 60 are indelibly scorched on the soil as a
red layer of burnt debris . . .

PETER MARSDEN, Roman London

O ne should be in no doubt about the dangerous nature of
the situation then facing the Romans in Britain. And
there was worse to come.

The Boudican revolt has been described as 'the most serious
rebellion against Roman rule in any province during the early
Principate' next to the great Batavian (Rhinelander) revolt under
Julius Civilis ten years later;[1] Julius Civilis being another
charismatic native leader of royal descent ill-treated by the
Romans – he was sent in irons to Rome – before he rebelled.
The Romans were experiencing for themselves the ugly truth, as
expressed by Tacitus, that they had broken the Britons into
obedience, 'but not as yet to slavery'.[2] Now that the habit of
obedience had been boldly flung off, the Britons were facing their
oppressors with all the banked energies of the unfairly subjugated, not the lethargy which long generations of serfdom can
breed. It was clear to the Romans themselves that such a British
onslaught, in equal measure surprising and horrifying, must be
checked and as soon as possible, lest the entire occupation of the
island be imperilled.

With the Roman commander at distant Anglesey, the nearest
available Roman force had to be flung into the fray, in order to
stop the British triumph at source, following the sack of
Camulodunum. That honour fell to the IXth Legion Hispana –
one of the legions which had taken part in the Claudian invasion,

taking its name from the Spanish province where it had served with distinction.[3] The commander of the IXth Legion, Petilius Cerialis, set off for Camulodunum with the intention of rescuing his compatriots, or at least of inflicting a smashing defeat upon the rebels. He probably came from a camp at Longthorpe, near Peterborough, some eighty miles from Colchester, and despite Tacitus' assertion, was not accompanied by a full legion, which would have comprised approximately five thousand men, but something under three thousand.[4]

If however the exact quantity of cohorts at Petilius' command is in doubt, their fate at the Britons' hands is not. Somewhere to the north of Camulodunum a British contingent was lying in wait: this would presumably have been a separate striking force from the army which had sacked the city and was probably detailed to cover just such a Roman advance. (We do not know precisely which tribes joined under Boudica, other than her own Iceni and the Trinovantes; some of the Coritani and the Cornovii from the Midlands were probably also there and maybe some disaffected Brigantes from further north; Dio's figure of 230,000 for Boudica's army at the final battle is obviously wildly exaggerated, but does at least convey the massive nature of the rising which Tacitus described as universal.)[5] The ambush was as bloodily successful as the sack of the city had been. Petilius' infantry was cut to pieces. He himself, according to Tacitus, escaped with his cavalry and took refuge back at the legionary camp.

Perhaps he had contributed to this defeat by acting rashly. Petilius' later career, which brought him into contact with that other native rebel, the Batavian Julius Civilis, showed him to be a general of daring rather than cautious instincts;[6] but at this point, while the Roman mentality still grappled bemusedly with the notion of British insurrection, caution would have been more desirable in a commander than daring. At least Petilius had survived to fight another day: and after his campaigns against Civilis he would end up as Governor of Britain. But for the present the Romans had now lost a further estimated 2,500 men, and were no nearer to stemming the British advance.

At this point, the Procurator Catus Decianus, he 'whose rapacity had driven the province to war' as Tacitus pointed out, exercised the traditional prerogative of the rat and fled the rapidly sinking ship. He took with him not only all his papers, but all his officers: Roman Britain was now without an administrative structure of any sort, and still the Governor Suetonius, hastening from Mona, had yet to arrive to save the situation – or so it was hoped.

Tacitus tells us that Suetonius was 'undismayed'. That was just as well. He certainly made excellent speed in his 250-mile dash towards Londinium since he managed to reach it in advance of the British hordes from Camulodunum (a mere sixty-three miles away).[7] Or perhaps the natural if damaging British concentration on plunder following the sack of the veterans' wealthy city was already weakening their original determination to extirpate the Roman rule. It was the element of surprise which had enabled the British tribal forces to slaughter Petilius' well-equipped and well-trained men of the IXth Legion. Since the Governor of Britain could hardly be expected to linger in western Mona once the startling news of the fall of Camulodunum reached him, it might have been as well for the Britons to employ the element of surprise once again, either by ambushing Petilius, or by occupying Londinium itself. But this was not to be.

So Suetonius reached Londinium unscathed, and reached it some short time ahead of the Britons; but it was an interval at least long enough for him to appraise the situation with his accustomed quick intelligence. Tacitus tells us that Suetonius had pressed on towards Londinium with the original intention of using it as a military stronghold. But it is important to realize, as Suetonius soon discovered, that Londinium at this point was not actually a fortified city. Nor for that matter was it the capital city of Roman Britain, a fact which may be difficult for twentieth-century Britons to appreciate, trained by long historical usage to think of London as the centre of their world at least, and perhaps of other worlds as well.

*

If not a military stronghold, what was the nature of the city to which Suetonius had hastened, and at which the marauding and triumphant Britons would soon arrive? Despite all the recent archaeological activity in this area, the exact origin of Londinium has not yet been established beyond all possibility of doubt.[8] Caesar does not mention Londinium at all in his account of the second (54 BC) campaign in the course of which he crossed the Thames; while it was the twelfth-century chronicler Geoffrey of Monmouth who was responsible for spreading the enduring legend of a pre-Roman city, something for which there is no support from archaeology. Since the name Londinium itself does derive from something pre-Roman, it was perhaps some obscure farm on a bend of the river which gave its name forever to the future mighty conurbation.[9]

Be that as it may, the archaeological evidence indicates that Londinium as known in the first century owed its foundation to the Romans. There are two main theories: the first suggests that Londinium was founded as a military base at the time of the Claudian invasion of 43. The second envisages it as 'a carefully planned civil trading settlement of Roman merchants'. It is the lack of military equipment among the discoveries unearthed which argues against the theory of the military base: unlike Colchester, for example, which is known to have been established in the first place as a fortification before being transformed into a *colonia*, and where a plethora of military remains have been turned up. The military argument cannot however be conclusively demolished. For one thing, the new settlement undeniably occupied a situation of strategic importance: it would make sense if its earliest Roman use was in fact as a place of river crossing, and that would suppose some form of military presence.[10]

The dating of the coins however suggests a town which began to flourish from about AD 50 onwards. Recent archaeological work has indeed tended to reinforce the notion of a town planned from the first and rapidly expanding. Traces of a major north-east–south-west Roman road have been revealed in Southwark, crossing the Thames just below the modern London Bridge (and above the mediaeval one). This is in addition to the long-known major east–west road, nine metres wide, which has been replaced by the modern Cheapside, but parts of which have been integrated into Lombard Street and Fenchurch Street. Traces of this north–south road, on the north bank of the Thames, were found in the winter of 1984/5 in King Street, between the Guildhall and St Paul's; already in the AD 50s it was attended by thriving shops.

There are also traces of a central square, probably a market square, under Gracechurch Street, as well as these broad roads, and although the Boudican destruction followed by Roman reconstruction makes it impossible to be certain, there may well have been an early temple; if so, it would notionally lie beneath the site of that temple, recently rediscovered, which is dated about AD 70. We know that there was at least one large building, a Roman version of a modern shopping mall; this had a deep verandah or portico running along in front of it, obviously intended for a series of different shops, which indicates that the Roman version of the developers were also present.

'Boudican' Londinium spread over thirty acres at least and may have had as many as thirty thousand inhabitants.[11] The limits of the city are indicated by various factors including, of course, those fire deposits which provide brutal evidence of how soon all this development was to be suddenly and violently shattered. The siting of the Roman cemeteries of this period is also important, since they had by law to lie outside the bounds of the city. Londinium in these early days would have centred round modern Lombard Street where it is bisected by Gracechurch Street, and continues into Fenchurch Street, with the findspots of shards and so forth heavily grouped near Leadenhall Market. A stream, later named the Walbrook, flowed through it, (its course lying beneath the modern Bank of England and Mansion House). The eastern limits of Londinium would have been not much further than Mincing Lane; the Fleet from which modern Fleet Street takes its name, then a navigable river, must have acted as a virtual boundary in the west.

Unlike hapless Camulodunum, the first British *colonia*, and the *municipium* of Verulamium to which Boudica's army would shortly turn its attentions, Londinium had as yet no official status. This is the description given to us by Tacitus: Londinium 'did not rank as a Roman settlement, but was an important centre for business-men and merchandise'. The word which Tacitus uses for businessmen, *negotiatores* – bankers or those engaged in financial transactions as opposed to *mercatores*, merchants – suggests incidentally that Londinium in its occupational use in AD 60 was not so far from that of the City of London, which now occupies more or less the same area.[12]

Although lacking a charter, the city may have enjoyed some kind of self-government under military control.[13] For whatever the origins of the site, it is clear that by AD 60 a teeming energetic cosmopolitan city, connected with Europe and beyond, full of confidence in its commercial future, occupied it. Londinium at this point should not be regarded as a 'British' city. It may have been temporarily swollen with British refugees, given the impending arrival of the Boudican army, already laying waste the countryside of the Thames between Camulodunum and their new target. But the city was not a natural focus for any particular British tribe, as the fact that it had taken a Roman foundation to conjure it into existence bears witness.[14]

The cosmopolitan nature of this busy community is on the contrary well illustrated by the kind of belongings and household objects it left behind, many of them luxuries which had to be imported from some far-flung town or country. Objects have been found as geographically diverse as red-pottery tableware from southern Italy, still showing traces of Vesuvian ash, amphorae, probably containing olive oil, from the Seville region of southern Spain, smaller amphorae for wine from Rhodes, and glassware from Syria. Here were wealthy merchants, already beginning to live in the kind of comfortable lifestyle they had enjoyed at home, not necessarily Roman, but from the easeful Mediterranean. As with Camulodunum, a growing body of expatriates had come to profit from the opportunities presented by the new Roman province, serenely confident that the graph of their prosperity must inevitably soar with the passage of time.

Then Suetonius arrived from Mona, took one look at Londinium and decided to abandon it to the enemy. The town, he believed, could not be defended and the horrifying recent experience of Petilius left him disinclined to emulate that commander's rashness; he was well aware of the inferior numbers of his own men compared to those of the Britons. It was better to live to fight another day. As Tacitus coolly and succinctly expressed it: 'He decided to save the whole situation by the sacrifice of a single city.' It was a radical and unsentimental solution.

In vain those about to be sacrificed – civilians all – prayed and wept not to be left to their fate. Suetonius gave the signal for departure. The brave Roman cavalry clattered away. The legionaries, those that there were, marched off. The able-bodied must have tried, many of them, to leave with him. At any rate, 'those who could keep up with him' were given a place. Others would have escaped up the waterway of the Thames to the safer territories of the Atrebates, with their capital at Silchester and their king Cogidubnus, like Cartimandua of the Brigantes, friendly to the Roman interests.[15] But there remained behind in Londinium, according to Tacitus, all those who could not travel, either because of their sex, or because they were too old (or, as he might have added, too young). And there was a third category, equally poignant from the point of view of the historian, of those who remained behind voluntarily because they were 'attached to the place'. Already it seems the city had its inveterate inhabitants, who if not native Britons, were in another sense already Londoners: these too stayed behind as centuries later Londoners would refuse to leave their homes during the Great Plague, the Great Fire and the Blitz.

'Never before or since has Britain ever been in a more disturbed and perilous state': records Tacitus, later, on the state of the Roman province at this time, and it is worth recalling that Tacitus had a first-hand witness to the events and emotions of that terrible period in his father-in-law, then a young man and a member of Suetonius' staff. With the veterans and their families massacred, a *colonia* burned to the ground, at least part of a Roman legion wiped out – a minimum of two thousand men – and now a populous merchant city abandoned, it is difficult to see that Tacitus was exaggerating.

Indeed, if the Boudican revolt was the second most serious provincial rising in this century, for a parallel to the Roman situation on the abandonment of Londinium it is suggested that one should go back a hundred years to Gaul.[16] Here the young champion of the Arverni, Vercingetorix, defeated Caesar at Gergovia in 52 BC, and at the head of a general army of the Gauls very nearly succeeded in throwing the Roman yoke off altogether.

The lamentations of the helpless inhabitants of Londinium had not been misplaced. Their city was to be destroyed and they themselves were to be sacrificed, in certain cases quite literally so. From the very first, serious excavations of the city of London – beginning in 1915 but with a rapid increase after the First World War – have indeed provided startling evidence of the violent demolition of an earlier foundation in the middle of the first century AD.[17]

The process of discovery, in connection with the building and rebuilding in this area, has continued in various phases ever since, with the depredations of the Blitz during the Second World War providing of course ripe opportunities. If not all of these were taken in the past – where archaeological discovery is concerned one might well adapt the words of Thomas Hood concerning a noted sportsman: 'What he hit is history; what he missed is mystery' – fortunately the present climate is increasingly favourable to co-operative ventures between archaeologist and developer.*

---

* Excavations of a site off Leadenhall Street during 1985–6 took place during a pause granted by the developer Legal & General before the erection of Leadenhall Court, a new centre of shops and offices; they were jointly supported by the Museum of London, English Heritage and the developer, who together formed the Roman Civic Centre Project.

In this way fragments of burned roofing tiles, wood ash conveniently accompanied by burned coins of the reign of Claudius – seventeen such bronze coins were discovered at a depth of seventeen feet when Lloyds Bank was built – burned grain from a merchant's stock he could not carry away, burned Samian ware, all these have provided mute testimony of the great fire which finally completed the holocaust of London. The civilized homes of the wealthy businessmen, made of timber and some clay, with their white plaster work, some of it decorated with colours, with their thatched roofs and their wooden floorboards, burned merrily. The elegant pots, the amphorae for the Greek wine and the Spanish oil, the decorated pottery lamps imported from the Mediterranean, all these witnesses to the sophisticated tastes of the first Londoners were first smashed by desecrating hands then baked in a furnace of destruction. The fact that some of these houses even had running water by this date would have been of little significance in view of the fiery furnace which now engulfed the centre of the city: it has been estimated from tests on burned Samian ware that the heat must have been in excess of $1,000°C$ (to be compared with the similarly estimated heat in the firestorms in Hamburg during the 1943 bombings, with all the additional aid of high explosives).[18]

Above all, more vivid to the eye than in the diagram and most vivid of all perhaps to the eye of the imagination, there is the red layer. Lying about thirteen feet below the surface and approximately sixteen inches deep, the red layer is the substratum of burned debris which serves as a perpetual reminder to the archaeologist of the severity of the Boudican attack. 'Far below the modern streets of the City of London', writes Peter Marsden, 'the events of AD 60 are indelibly scorched on the soil . . .'[19]

The massacred inhabitants have left no equivalent red layer. As with Camulodunum, where, as has been seen, similar conditions of fire and slaughter prevailed, we can presume that the Romans returned to the smoking ruins – or perhaps long after they had grown cold, for the time scale of all these events remains mysterious – and gave the wretched victims a mass cremation.

There are no skeletons, skulls or mere bones which can be ascribed to the first-century sacking with the same conviction as can for example the Samian ware baked black or the hoard of burned bronze coins in the foundations of Lloyds Bank.

If there can be no certainty, there are nevertheless some grisly relics which have been interpreted as coming from the Boudican era, since their actual form – skulls of heads which had been hacked off the body – fits plausibly into the known pattern of Celtic tribal practice.[20] Some of these decapitated skulls may have been discovered in the Walbrook stream as early as mediaeval times: Geoffrey of Monmouth's story of the mass beheading of a legion on its banks at the orders of Allectus, who led a revolt at the end of the third century, was perhaps an imaginative response to their persistent appearance as wells were being dug. In recent years at least 140 skulls have been turned up on four sites around the crucial Walbrook area, with references to a possible further large number on a fifth site. In no case have skeletons or other bones been found adjacent to these skulls.

There are various possible explanations for such large-scale finds. Since the earliest cemeteries – those just outside the city limits – are not far from the Walbrook area, these vagabond skulls might in theory have somehow been swept by the stream from their original sites, although it has been pointed out that the Walbrook even in its prime was never particularly fast-flowing. Furthermore it seems a strange coincidence that only the skulls were displaced. The skulls certainly belong to the early Roman period, first or second centuries, with at least one of them embedded in a wall erected in 200. It is surely legitimate therefore to connect them, however tentatively, with the one large-scale massacre known to have taken place within Londinium at this time, one moreover conducted by tribes with an historically known taste for the ritual use of water, wells, groves and streams in worship, and the ritual involvement of the head – both in life and death.[21]

Despite the absence of physical relics, Tacitus leaves us in no doubt that an immense number of people died at the hands of the

Boudican armies. It is true that his estimated figure of seventy thousand Roman and provincial dead, counting the sack of Verulamium yet to come, is once again likely to be an exaggeration. But actual figures in these matters, even if verifiable, have a way of being secondary to the impact of the event itself. (For instance, the Cromwellian massacre at Drogheda killed three thousand Irish according to the official verdict, four thousand at most: it is hardly necessary to emphasize the resonance of *that* event down the ages.)[22] It is the overall picture of an 'indescribable slaughter' taking place, as perceived by the Romans, remembered by the surviving witnesses, which is both appalling and convincing.

Nor do Tacitus and Dio combined spare us concerning the atrocious manner in which many of these victims died. In the *Agricola*, Tacitus merely makes a general statement that 'there was no form of savage cruelty that the angry victors refrained from'; in the *Annals* however he explains further that the Britons never thought it worthwhile to take prisoners in order to sell them (as was sometimes done at the time) or to exchange them for their own men. On the contrary: 'They could not wait to cut throats, hang, burn, and crucify . . .' Dio's account is even more specific and as a result even more dreadful.[23]

'Those who were taken captive by the Britons were subjected to every known outrage', he wrote. 'The worst and most bestial atrocity committed by their captors was the following. They hung up naked the noblest and most distinguished women and then cut off their breasts and sewed them to their mouths, in order to make the victims appear to be eating them; afterwards they impaled the women on sharp skewers run lengthwise through the entire body.' On one level, the symbolism of these skewers with which the formerly oppressed tortured and killed the womenfolk of the former oppressors is sufficiently obvious, if horribly so. But Dio makes the point that these obscene cruelties were also accompanied by 'sacrifices, banquets' and what he calls 'wanton behaviour' which took place in the Britons' sacred places, and in particular in the grove of Andate, their goddess of Victory whom they regarded with 'most exceptional reverence'. Taking Boudica's earlier invocation to the Iceni goddess Andraste (or Andaste) 'as woman speaking to woman' and putting it together with this mention of Andate and her sacred groves, it would seem that the general slaughter practised by the Britons had some distinctly religious or ritual element attached to it; as did the Iceni rising, with a Holy (Armed) Figurehead at its head.

The presence of a ritual element does not of course palliate the fact of the slaughter – or the atrocities which accompanied it; on the other hand it should not make them seem worse. It is natural of course for a later age, sharing neither the religious obsessions nor the oppression which had provoked the rebellion, to shrink back in horror from details such as Dio's. Tacitus' explanation for these cruelties is however a significant one: the Britons must have had a premonition of what was going to happen to them: they acted 'as though avenging, in advance, the retribution that was on its way'. As will be seen, he relates the Romans' own final full-scale slaughter of the Britons, including their women and their very baggage animals – 'transfixed with weapons' – without emotion; no need is felt here to explain let alone justify such ferocity. The Romans were the winners, and the implacable destruction of the losers was their right and even, it might be argued, their duty.

For Roman civilization itself was far from lacking the concept of revenge. The most celebrated temple in all Rome was that dedicated at the turn of the last century BC to the god of vengeance, Mars Ultor. (While in Mars' wife Bellona the Romans had their own ferocious chariot-driving spear-waving goddess of war, to whom future Warrior Queens would sometimes be compared, or compare themselves.)[24] This temple was dedicated by Augustus after the battle of Philippi when he considered that he had avenged the murder of Caesar: here magpies and vultures and larger victims, horses and wolves, were sacrificed on the bloodstained altars. If it is argued – inverting Tacitus as it were – that the Romans in Britain after Boudica's defeat were merely avenging what had gone before, then it must be pointed out that

Roman history was certainly not deficient in instances when hapless civilians had been massacred. Returning once again to the comparison with Vercingetorix, Caesar, for example, put all the innocent inhabitants of Avaricum (Bourges) to the sword during the period of his wars against the Gallic leader.

It has been remarked more than once that at the hands of the Romans the weak had no rights.[25] Momentarily under Boudica, the Britons – like the Indians at the time of the Mutiny in 1857, to which we will return – had ceased to be the weak. Zestfully, they did not hesitate to take full advantage of their new strength. Where historical massacres are concerned, twinkling as they do like innumerable black stars in the moral galaxy of history, it seems fairest to divide them into two categories: those where the oppressed rise up and strike down their oppressors, exacting vengeance in the process, and those where the rulers or invaders exact their own vengeance on a particular section of the population, for their own reasons. The Boudican vengeance fell into the former category, which has at least the merit of being the more comprehensible of the two.

Curiously enough, Boudica's own reputation as the leader who headed this avenging force has remained remarkably free of the taint of atrocity. Boadicea, as she must now become in reference to her later reputation, is frequently seen as a partisan queen of considerable nobility. Her lethal scythe-wheeled chariot also features more often than not – the chariot that never was – but somehow Boadicea herself never seems to leap down from it to take part in the bloodstained termination of a Roman civilian life. This may well be accurate, and again it may not. The highly limited sources available neither implicate Boudica personally in the bloodshed nor defend her from it. History – legend – has however by implication defended her from the charge of atrocity by glossing over it where she herself is concerned.

Beneath this lies the incontrovertible fact of Boadicea's feminine gender. It is as though a woman leader can mount a ritual chariot, wave a metaphorical banner in the air, invoke the spirits of revenge in return for intolerable wrongs done to her, but she must not actually be involved in the killing itself. After all, if there is no direct evidence that she was so involved, there is also no evidence against it. Boudica at all points cheered on the Britons and urged them to defeat the Romans. So the well-attested massacres – as well attested as any other part of the story of Boudica, since both Tacitus and Dio report them – vanish in favour of the patriotic female leader on high in her chariot: high that is, morally as well as physically, above the inevitable consequences of her oratory.

There is an appropriateness about this, which does not necessarily relate to historical truth. Boudica's sex and that of her children made them peculiarly vulnerable targets to the Romans, intent on making a series of symbolically brutal gestures to indicate the uselessness of British resistance. So Boadicea's sex has subsequently saved her legend from the tarnish of Dio's revelations, for which in fact as the effective leader of the Britons she must have been morally if not physically responsible.

Meanwhile the red layer beneath the City of London serves as a different kind of *memento mori* of the Boudican sacking and perhaps a more pertinent one. Its existence is a perpetual reminder that even the most thriving commercial city can be laid low, and that by a people generally despised as slaves, and that all in an instant of time: the destruction of everything made of clay, timber, thatch – or even other, far more durable modern materials – is guaranteed.

For afterwards, after Boudica and her troops had streamed on to enjoy one further fevered hour of triumph before tuning towards oblivion – as it seemed – Londinium too fell into a state of decay and became a kind of ghost town. (Even the great new roads north of the river were abandoned: those newly excavated in the King Street site show a period of about twenty years' disuse.)[26] In the nineteenth century Macaulay imagined a situation in which some kind of 'malady' would be engendered within 'the bosom of civilization itself' to bring about the collapse of the then flourishing city of London: 'is it possible that, in two or three hundred years, a few lean and half-naked fishermen may divide the ruins . . . with owls and foxes, may wash their nets amid the relics of her gigantic docks, and build their huts out of the capitals of her stately cathedrals?'[27]

But in the middle of the first century AD it had already happened.

CHAPTER SEVEN

Eighty Thousand Dead

It was a glorious victory, comparable with bygone triumphs.
According to one report, almost eighty thousand Britons
fell.

TACITUS, Annals

After the fall of Londinium, there was still a third city to be
sacrificed. Not yet gorged with slaughter or, more to the
point, plunder, the Britons under Boudica swept on to
Verulamium (St Albans). The city was not defended. Suetonius,
the Roman commander who had coolly appraised the necessity
of deserting an entire expatriate community, was not likely to
hesitate over the fate of Verulamium. This was primarily because
Suetonius' attention remained focused on those measures likely
to stave off Roman defeat in the first place, and then turn the
whole pulsating British advance to the Roman advantage: it was
after all for the long-term victory, or at least the saving of the
province, that he had taken the decision to abandon Londinium.

At the same time Verulamium as a city was quite different in
kind from both Camulodunum and Londinium. It was populated
neither by Roman veterans and their families nor by Mediterranean businessmen but by Britons – albeit Britons friendly to the
cause of Rome. Tacitus tells us categorically that Verulamium by
this date had been granted *municipium* status, which ranked it
below a veteran's settlement (a *colonia*) but above an ordinary
native tribal town (a *civitas*).

This privileged status must have had its roots in the events of
the Claudian invasion in 43 when the Catuvellauni, in whose
territory lay the town of Verulamium, had acted helpfully towards
the Roman cause. Certainly Tacitus' testimony is born out by

archaeology. A Belgic stronghold called Verlamio had antedated
Verulamium on the same site, but excavations (by Sir Mortimer
Wheeler and later Sheppard Frere) have revealed that a carefully
planned new British city was laid out from about AD 49 onwards.
Furthermore, traces of a country house, a villa made of timber at
Gorhambury, reveal that the loyal – to the Romans – Britons at
Verulamium were beginning to live as did their new masters and
allies.[1]

As Verulamium's privileged status harked back to the events of
43, so the rivalries and hatreds of its inhabitants' fellow Britons
must also have played their part in the destruction which
followed. A favourite notoriously has no friends. There was little
sympathy and much jealousy to inspire the horde which now
swooped down on its third municipal victim (Dio suggests that
only two cities were laid waste but, since he does not name them,
Tacitus' testimony of three, bearing in mind his connection to the
eyewitness, Agricola, is to be preferred). The fine Gorhambury
villa was jealously destroyed by fire, as was much of the rest of the
town.[2]

Once again excavations have provided evidence of a red layer
of burned daub and ash far below modern St Albans: three shops
disinterred from 1955 onwards give the same impression of
normal busy life rudely interrupted, a first-century time warp, as
has already been noted at Colchester and London. The modern
focus of historical attention is however the later Christian town:
the Roman city which was resurrected after the Boudican sack is
now the site of a car park and an ornamental lake; the relics of the
Roman theatre which can be inspected nearby are witness more
to this placid prosperous centre than to the British *municipium*
which the Queen of the Iceni and others in her army set on fire.
Early British Verulamium has left little trace compared to these
glamorous later developments.

But if there is evidence of fire, the same proportion of charred
personal belongings has not survived. The fate of the residents of
Camulodunum and Londinium served as an awful warning to the
Britons of Verulamium; they had no wish to share it. These more

fortunate citizens were able to make their getaway well in advance.

Once again Tacitus is clear on this point: 'The natives enjoyed plundering and thought of nothing else. Bypassing forts and garrisons, they made for where the loot was richest and protection weakest.' Even if one allows for Tacitus' natural tendency to emphasize the superiority of the Romans, it must be admitted that Boudica – or whoever actually decided the direction of the British army under her titular command – had made a strategic mistake in ignoring for the second time the need to strike at Suetonius while he was at his most vulnerable.

For all Suetonius' rapid and ruthless retreat from Londinium, he remained at risk until he had secured reinforcements for his own small force. This urgent need for reinforcements provides indeed the strongest argument for the theory that Suetonius must now have turned back to the Midlands and away from the London area. (The sources give us neither a specific geographical setting nor a time scale for the crucial events following the sack of Verulamium and leading up to the so-called 'last battle' between Romans and Britons.) The principal asset of the Boudican army was its size, enormous if now unquantifiable, but doubtless swollen with each successful foray, as the local tribes increasingly came to see the British side as the winning one. Then there was that famous Celtic courage, rashness if you like, which was particularly effective in surprise attacks and ambushes. Both these assets were liable to diminish as Suetonius caught up with his desired reinforcements, seasoned troops, and the British numerical superiority declined. And an element of surprise in the British attack could obviously not be long preserved, certainly not long enough for the Britons to gorge themselves in a further feast of municipal plunder along the way.

As it was, Suetonius had to face yet another reverse, this time one dealt out to him by his own side. Suetonius' plans for bolstering up his own numbers from among the various legions scattered about the province included summoning the IInd Legion Augusta – so called because it had been raised by the

Emperor – whose base was in the south-west at Exeter. The designated meeting place would have been modern Wroxeter (then known as Viroconium) or somewhere thereabouts in the West Midlands. Unfortunately Poenius Postumus, the Roman commander in charge of the IInd Legion – his actual title was *praefectus castrorum,* that is, camp commandant – failed to bring his men to the appointed rendezvous.

Poenius Postumus' reasons for ignoring the summons are unknown: he may even have been pinned down by another tribe and had no choice in the matter. But his failure to arrive certainly increased. Suetonius' problems. Lacking the men of the IInd Augusta, the latter was left to pull together the XIVth Legion and a detachment of the XXth (these had been with him on the Mona expedition) and the nearest auxiliaries available; out of all these Suetonius welded together a force of men variously estimated at between ten and fifteen thousand. Even if Dio's estimated figure of 230,000 for the Boudican army is reduced to a hundred thousand or less, Suetonius' troops must still have been heavily outnumbered. On the other hand these were hardened fighting men.[3]

Under the circumstances, Suetonius decided to attack the Britons without further delay. The bold decision that Boudica – or her deputies – should perhaps have taken themselves was in fact taken by the Roman Governor. This at any rate is Tacitus' version of events, and it fits with what we already know of Suetonius' character and his approach to strategy. He needed every advantage he could get against the numerically unequal odds; to choose the site of the battle himself and thus by implication its timing was to award himself two vital ones – as indeed it proved. It is true that Dio suggests to the contrary that the battle was imposed upon Suetonius against his better judgement as his legionaries grew short of food and the barbarians pressed him. But once again, Tacitus' access to Agricola means that in a contradiction of this sort, especially over matters of military detail, his version takes priority. Furthermore Tacitus is convincingly explicit about the terrain chosen by Suetonius – without unfortunately naming it: 'a position in a defile with a wood behind him'. This meant, as Suetonius realized, that he would only have to face an enemy at his front and here there was 'open country without cover for ambushes'. These details smack of actual decisions taken and recollected in tranquillity long after.

Much ink has been spilt over the site of Boudica's last battle, figuratively as well as actually, since it continues to be spilt in what might be described as the post-ink age. With Dio passing over the subject altogether – he tells us nothing at all about the actual site of the battle, not even the nature of its terrain – and Tacitus confining himself to the physical characteristics quoted above, an atmosphere had prevailed in which supposition, proposition and opposition have all been able to flourish happily. (In the 1980s two scholarly disputants concerning the location of the site did agree about one thing, that 'the search for the pattern of the Boudica campaign is great fun'.)[4] The key question must remain the view taken of Suetonius' movements after his departure from Londinium, and during and after the sack of Verulamium.

It if is accepted that Suetonius went in search of reinforcements in those areas – basically to the west – where the scattered legionary fortresses and garrison could most easily succour his limited force, and then chose the position for the engagement for which he was now himself prepared, then a convincing argument can and has been put forward for a West Midlands site.[5]

In centuries gone by, however, a romantic attachment was felt to the notion of a last battle in London itself with special heed given to the area around King's Cross station, built in 1852 and for which the name Boadicea's Cross was at one point even proposed. The name Battle Bridge for an old crossing of the Fleet river near King's Cross was held optimistically to offer encouragement. Thomas Nelson, author of *The History of Islington*, printed in 1811, was among antiquaries who were attracted by the idea of locating thereabouts 'the operations of the Roman

General in his arduous contest with that injured and unfortunate Princess'. In his long but spirited biography of 1937, *Boadicea*, Lewis Spence took much trouble, by the use of ancient contour maps, to point out the existence of some kind of defile around York Road and the Caledonian Road, between the 'acclivity' of Pentonville and the high ground near Gray's Inn Land.[6]

Nor has London and its environs been allowed to dominate the field entirely: other suggested localities have included Wheathampstead, while Ambersbury Banks, a large earthwork in Epping Forest, is among local sites where the tradition of the last battle is cherished. Moreover in 1983 a revisionist argument for the Staines area was put forward by Nicholas Fuentes in the *London Archaeologist*; concentrating on the age-old valley between the well-wooded Shrubs Hill and the River Thames, and placing the 'defile' approximately where Virginia Water station is today. This argument however demands a radical reassessment of Suetonius' campaign following Mona, including the theory that he actually brought his entire task force to Londinium, not merely his cavalry; it also proposed that Cogidubnus and the Atrebates of the Silchester area were somehow involved in the last battle; in the absence of firm new archaeological evidence, all this seems a revision too far.[7]

So for the time being at least the West Midlands region remains the most plausible locality, one supported by the known deployment of the Roman military forces around AD 60, the forces upon which Suetonius now drew, as Tacitus quite clearly tells us. Attention has been focused in particular on the Warwickshire area north-west of Nuneaton, near Atherstone; here, at Mancetter (Roman Manduessum), a steep escarpment can be seen rising from the plain. The discovery and exploration of a Roman camp here, which was the site of the xiv[th] Legion until it moved up to Wroxeter in about AD 55, has underlined its claims as a possible site of the last battle. Although the xiv[th] Legion would have departed by the time of the Boudican rebellion, auxiliary units – trained non-Roman troops – would presumably have still used the camp, and that would have made

Manduessum, coupled with its terrain (still today conforming quite markedly to Tacitus' description), an ideal focus for Suetonius' strategic plan. * It would of course take the discovery of 'some quite remarkable finds . . . such as a mass burial with closely identifiable weapons in association' for the status of Mancetter/Manduessum to be finally verifiable.[8] In the meantime no more plausible alternative has been put forward.

If the site of the last battle is finally unknown and perhaps unknowable, the course of the battle presents a different problem. One travels back in time from the suppositions of the twentieth-century archaeologists – agreeing only on the lack of certainty possible and the 'fun' involved in the discussion – to the ancient historians, who express their respective certainties by once again contradicting each other, as they do over Suetonius' role in its inception. Once again, and for the same reason, Tacitus' is the preferred account.

There was one matter on which the two ancient historians did agree – that the battle itself was preceded by a series of set speeches. But as with Dio's earlier Boudican speech, recounted in Chapter Five, this was more a question of contemporary protocol than historical accuracy. In this case Tacitus and Dio give us a total of three speeches: one apiece for Boudica and Suetonius from Tacitus; Dio, having already given the Queen her say, contents himself with awarding Suetonius a tripartite speech, delivered in turn to his three divisions. It is Tacitus' portrait of the Queen on this occasion, driving round and round the assembled tribes in her chariot, with her daughters in front of her, which has made an indelible impression. It has become joined to that physical description given by Dio on the earlier occasion of the tall, splendid and ferocious red-haired Celt in her war panoply; together they form the popular image of Boadicea.

'We British are used to women commanders in war' the Queen

---

* Nowadays the London–Manchester InterCity railway line passes through the site of the battle; the historically minded traveller may salute the memory of the Queen of the Iceni from the windows of the train.

cries, before adding, with that neat lack of logic many other Warrior Queens will be found to echo: 'I am descended from mighty *men*!' Otherwise Tacitus' Boudica emphasizes her ghastly treatment at the hands of the Romans – 'I am fighting as an ordinary person for my lost freedom, my bruised body and my outraged daughters' – and dwells further on other Roman atrocities, as well as denigrating the Roman courage. She ends with this clarion call to invoke – like so many Warrior Queens – a sense of masculine shame: 'consider how many of you are fighting – and why. Then you will win this battle, or perish. That is what I, a woman, plan to do! Let the men live in slavery if they will.'

Suetonius, according to Tacitus, also stressed the feminine presence in the British ranks, but in this case he did so only in order to hold it to scorn: 'In their ranks there are more women than fighting men.' Dio's Suetonius equally took the opportunity to sneer at the natives: 'Fear not, then, their numbers or their spirit of rebellion; for their boldness rests on nothing more than headlong rashness unaided by arms or training!' The Britons' achievement in capturing the two cities of Camulodunum and Londinium is dismissed as being due to betrayal in one case and abandonment in the other. With the confidence of a member of the master race, Dio's Suetonius declares: 'let them learn by actual experience the difference between us, whom they have wronged, and themselves'.

The rightness of the Roman cause is indeed one of the major themes of Dio's Suetonius: 'the gods are our allies', he goes on to say to this third division, 'for they almost always side with those who have been wronged'. His other theme is the natural superiority of their heritage: 'we are Romans and have triumphed over all mankind by our valour'. Lastly Dio's Suetonius does at least envisage the possibility of defeat, if only to allow the author to dwell once again on those British atrocities which he had already described so vividly apropos the women sacrificed to Andate. If the Romans did not triumph and were captured, they could expect to be impaled, to look upon their own entrails cut from their bodies, to be spitted on red-hot skewers, to be melted in boiling water . . . In a word, 'to suffer as though . . . thrown to lawless and impious beasts'.

In the event Suetonius' confidence was justified: except that the courage was found equally on both sides, the skill and experience solely on that of the Romans. Even before battle was joined, the two armies drawn up for battle would have presented an extraordinary contrast in their equipment and the manner of their array, a contrast which only became more intense as the conflict proceeded.

Here were the Britons, a vast concourse of them it is true, but in no sense a standing army: the fact that they were farmers, that they had literally come off the land, would be cruelly emphasized in the aftermath to the battle. The Celtic sword was the traditional weapon of such people, a sword with a long history, a sword such as the sword with which 'the wild deer', Cúchulainn, had been able to despatch all fourteen soldiers sent after him by the wicked Queen Medb. They wore no body armour of any sort, except perhaps a pair of loose trousers (if we judge by the Gauls depicted on the Roman sculptural reliefs). The fine helmets and decorated shields which this civilization has left behind were for the aristocrat–warriors among them: these too would have been mounted on the light wickerwork chariots, like to their queen's, from which they habitually dismounted to fight. (The chariot was however already slightly old-fashioned and had vanished altogether from the British/Celtic host by the second century AD.)[9]

We may believe that this concourse had the noisy, shambling quality of the Celtic array, with its music and its shouting and some hoarse amalgamation of the two. Perhaps the most significant difference of all between the British army and the one which faced it within the defile was that the Britons had brought along their families to see the fun. There they were, women and children, in a series of wagons stationed at the edge of the battlefield – which meant, given the lie of the land, at the back of it. One imagines a certain boastfulness in the mounted warriors of the Britons, and in their foot followers too, as beneath the eyes of their dependants they 'seethed over a wide area in unprecedented numbers'. The presence of these innocent camp followers, in a position which might well and in fact did prove extraordinarily dangerous, illustrates perfectly how war for the Britons, with its joy of fighting, its hope of plunder, was a serious but also a tribal business.

For the Romans on the opposite side, war was not only a serious business but the only business. It was for this that the legionaries had been trained, trained in many cases over long years and in the hard school of continental warfare; above all it was for this business of fighting that they were equipped, and equipped in a manner which was developed further each decade with the sole aim of making every legion a superb fighting machine. Against their naked or near naked opponents, they wore helmets including neck protection, light body armour to the waist, broad leather belts with metal-tipped leather thongs falling below them, and studded open boots like hobnailed sandals.[10]

When it came to weaponry, the Roman cavalry had their lances, while the infantry, as well as curved wooden shields with bosses, had a pair of javelins per man. These javelins were seven feet long with a three-foot iron point, difficult to remove once embedded: but their long wooden shafts made them easy to throw. With the aid of his javelin, the legionary could render his opponent's shield useless, or even pin the two of them together. Furthermore a legionary also had a shorter two-foot sword (his *gladius*, hence *gladiator*) and a dagger. It was the long hero's sword of Cúchulainn against a battery of professional weapons. But the legionaries of Rome were not to be equated with the soldiers of Queen Medb. Alas, this was not a contest which the epic hero — or heroine — was destined to win.

At the first charge of the Britons towards the defile which contained their enemy, the Roman legionaries deliberately held their ground without counterattacking, as they had been trained to do. But when the order finally came to burst forward with their lethal javelins, they did so in wedge formation and to murderous effect, accompanied by the infantry of the auxiliaries. Finally it was the cavalry's turn to demolish all resistance. We do not know how long the battle raged – all day? less than that? The duration was of less significance than the final result.

The Britons, by dreadful irony, found themselves pinned in against this fierce counterattack by their own wagons, those wagons brought along so blithely for their families to see the show. It was in this way, in this death-trap, that the Romans were able to put to death the British women, as well as the British baggage animals (which were transfixed) at the same time as they despatched their menfolk. 'According to one report,' says Tacitus carefully, eighty thousand of the Britons died, compared to four hundred Romans killed, and others wounded.

Was Queen Boudica herself to be numbered among the eighty thousand British dead? The indications are that she did not actually die on the battlefield, but shortly afterwards and by her own hand: Tacitus tells us that she took poison. (Dio's story that Boudica fell sick and then died is not incompatible with this, since poison would obviously have brought about sickness, however short-lived, and it may have been this aspect of the story which Dio picked up.) As for the Queen's daughters, their fate, like their names, remains unknown to history since it is not mentioned by Tacitus, while their very existence is ignored by Dio.

For once, however, the many fictional accounts of Boadicea's life, be they plays or novels, which have her administering poison to her daughters as well as to herself, are not straining credulity too far. In Beaumont and Fletcher's play, for example, the heroine's younger daughter momentarily shrinks back from the mystery of death – 'O but if I knew but whither . . .' – as her mother offers her the fatal draught. The Queen comforts her and issues her last rallying cry:

> Keep your minds humble, your devotions high
> So shall ye learn the noblest part, to die.[11]

For if the Iceni princesses did survive the wanton slaughter at the end of the battle, it is surely not likely that their mother, having decided to poison herself, would have risked them falling into the hands of the Romans – a second time.

As it is, myth surrounds Queen Boudica's burial place as with everything else about her. Dio tells us simply that the British gave her a costly burial, Tacitus nothing. The seventeenth-century story that Boadicea (as she now becomes) was given this 'costly burial' at Stonehenge has a great deal to commend it of neatness and romance – if nothing of historical truth – since two mighty legends are disposed of together, the immemorial stones and the woman. The celebrated if equally unhistorical connection of the Druids with Stonehenge only dates in fact from the later years of the seventeenth century: in 1624 for example, the antiquary Edmund Bolton, believing Stonehenge to be the work of Britons ('the rudeness itself persuades'), concluded that here was to be found the tomb of Boadicea. This theory was rebutted in 1655 in a posthumous publication from notes by Inigo Jones. He pointed out that 'a mighty Prince may be buried with great Solemnity, yet no material Monument be dedicated to his memory'; adding that it was unlikely the Romans would have permitted 'an everlasting Remembrance of Boadicea'.[12] (Although the Romans had in fact a tradition of allowing their enemies to carry away their dead for burial – to avoid evil spirits – so that the erection of 'an everlasting Remembrance' was not out of the question in Iceni country.)

To many other neighbourhoods and many other monuments, however man-made or otherwise, clings obstinately the tradition that 'Here lies Boadicea'. Counted among them are a mound on Hampstead Heath known as Boadicea's Tomb (in reality more likely to be a Roman burial place); various sites around Parliament Hill, following the legend of the London King's Cross battle; Warlies Park, Waltham Abbey, in Essex; the Bartlow Hills in the same county; and a tumulus known locally as The Bubberies in the grounds of a parsonage at Quidenham in Norfolk – the name being hopefully regarded as a corruption of Boadicea or Boudica. The legend of the King's Cross battle is also responsible for periodic bursts of enthusiasm (most recently in 1988), suggesting that the British Queen must lie buried under Platform 8 of the station itself, a story which may at least divert the weary traveller, causing him or her to ruminate on the possible advantages of the chariot over the train as a means of conveyance.[13] The discovery of a mid-first-century British burial place, containing the bones of a woman of royal rank, would be exciting enough in its own right; it would also, for better or for worse, put an end to such innocent local fantasies.

Whatever the truth of the costly burial and its precise situation – and as with the royal palace of the Iceni, one must not give up all hope of finding it within the tribal area – it is reasonable to assume that Queen Boadicea took her own life. Let us suppose that the Emperor Nero did choose to exercise clemency towards this barbarian princess, once she had served her purpose in the triumphal procession (as Claudius had exercised clemency towards Caratacus). Let us suppose that the offer was made, and the Iceni Queen believed that the promise would be kept. She would not have wished to live out her days a slave. Shakespeare's description of Cleopatra not wishing to see 'some squeaking Cleopatra . . . boy her greatness' on the Roman stage would surely have been paralleled by Boudica's own profound wish not to experience further humiliation.

There were royal 'slaves' who settled down in Rome – Queen Zenobia of Palmyra will provide an interesting example of such in the following chapter; there were also the barbarian captives described by Gibbon: 'taken in thousands by the chance of war, purchased at a vile price, accustomed to a life of independence, and impatient to break and revenge their fetters'.[14] Everything we know about Boudica, one certainly accustomed to a life of independence, suggests that she would have fallen proudly into the latter category. As for slavery, there is of course also no guarantee that she would have been offered that option. It is true that the womenfolk of Caratacus had been well treated following his ritual exhibition in a Roman triumph. But Caesar earlier had executed Vercingetorix after a similar display. Caratacus' womenfolk were also women who had acted within the Roman meaning of the word: they had not challenged the might of Rome successfully. Boudica, who had already experienced Roman brutality before ever she rebelled, had no reason to suppose that the penalties which followed it would be any less severe. As the Queen herself was made to exclaim by Tacitus: for her as a woman it was a case of winning this battle or perishing. She had not won; we must therefore believe that she kept her word and perished.

The vengeance of Suetonius against the Britons was every bit as frightful as that of the rebel Britons had been towards Rome. (A further convincing argument for the death of Boudica shortly after the end of the battle lies in the fact that she would otherwise surely have featured in it.) The British must have suffered shockingly, and not all of the victims had taken part in the rising. For not only those who were judged hostile but those who were deemed to be 'wavering' were 'ravaged with fire and sword': the latter category, being in the eye of the Roman beholder, could encompass almost everybody and justify many a retributive cruelty. Even more terrible were the Britons' sufferings from famine, for the Iceni in particular had neglected to sow their own fields before departing on their victorious rampage, taking everyone with them: the cheerful intention had been to seize the Roman supplies.

Some of the Britons went on fighting. Confusion has arisen about their desperate continuance of the struggle which was manifestly lost, and there is a suggestion that it was bound up with the implacability of Suetonius towards those who had recently humiliated him by ravaging the province under his command.[15] This is Tacitus' story in the earlier of his two accounts, the *Agricola*: 'Excellent officer though he [Suetonius] was, it was feared that he would abuse their surrender and punish every offence with undue severity, as if it were a personal injury.' So some of them fought on, feeling that at this point they had nothing to lose.

In the later *Annals*, however, Tacitus linked this ultimate British stand to the mischievous influence of the new Procurator, Julius Classicianus, he who came to replace the fugitive Catus

Decianus. Julius Classicianus disloyally hinted that it was in the Britons' own interest to prolong their activities until a new or less personally involved – and thus milder – governor should be sent out from Rome. Whether Tacitus' slur on Julius Classicianus' loyalty is justified, or whether he was merely seeking to defend the reputation of his father-in-law's old commander, it is true that a 'milder' governor was finally sent out from Rome: Publius Petronius Turpilianus, who had just finished being Consul. This followed a report by the Emperor Nero's emissary, the former slave Polyclitus, who tried to reconcile Governor and Procurator, and ended by criticizing Suetonius for not terminating the war. Peace was finally restored. With peace however came repression.

If the execution of the Roman vengeance lacked those picturesque atrocities depicted by Dio (so far as we know) it partook of the equally grim nature of long-drawn-out persecution including whatever brutal measures were thought necessary under the circumstances. Fresh troops were brought from Germany to fill out the ranks of that legion brought low by the first British onslaught; auxiliaries, both infantry and cavalry, were also imported. The Iceni paid dearly for their crowded hour of glorious life, and were condemned to live out instead that traditional alternative to it, a dismal age without a name. Excavations of the post-Boudican age reveal that a detailed policy of repression was enacted towards the guilty tribe, including slavery and transportation. Temporary Roman forts were put up at strategic sites for the control of the population, such as Great Chesterford north of Saffron Walden, Coddenham near Ipswich and Pakenham near Ixworth on the borders of Suffolk and Norfolk.* 16

Farms were burned, sanctuaries such as that of Arminghall desecrated; some of the buried hoards of torcs, coins and other

---

* From time to time traces of these forts, symbolic of the repression of the Iceni, emerge as a result of drought and aerial photography: in this way the Roman camp at Pakenham was shown up in 1976, and excavated in 1985 before being engulfed by a bypass.

precious golden objects referred to in Chapter Four, such as that at Santon, may owe their origins to this terrible time. The draining of hitherto unoccupied territories in the Iceni area and the conversion of them into fertile land was probably carried out by deported Iceni slave labour (using Roman drainage systems). So the Iceni, proud and independent of yore, were made subject, and this time they did not revolt again. The evidence is that in punishment for their rebellion the Iceni lands remained wasted into the next century. To the Caledonian leader Calgacus, via the pen of Tacitus, went the last word, when he was raising his own rebellion (put down by Agricola) in the 80s. Of the Romans, he said 'they create a desolation and call it peace'.[17]

So Britain as a whole settled down to be a Roman province: or as the unknown but free-spirited Briton inspecting from an observation point some excavations of the Roman period at Leadenhall Court in the City of London observed to the present writer in 1986, 'That's the Romans for you – four hundred years of occupying *our* country.'

Were these four hundred years of occupation inevitable (leaving aside the question of whether they were desirable)? How far did Queen Boudica of the Iceni really progress in the direction of eliminating that occupation? The Romans in Britain trembled and with good reason, but what about the imperial power itself? Did Rome tremble? Should it have done so? The answers to these questions, fascinating if finally imponderable, are linked in part to Tacitus' own estimate of Suetonius' achievement.

Tacitus quoted the last battle as being 'a glorious victory' for the Roman side, 'comparable with bygone triumphs'. Poenius Postumus, that senior officer who had failed to answer Suetonius' summons to a rendezvous, subsequently fell on his sword because he had robbed his own legion of the possibility of sharing in all this glory. If Suetonius really triumphed with great difficulty over Boudica – against overwhelming odds as well as overwhelming numbers – then the Iceni, and the other tribes who joined with them, must have nearly succeeded in their objective, the overturning of odious Roman rule.

Against this picture of Boudica having suffered a last-minute reverse due to the military cunning of Suetonius and the experienced, courageous brilliance of his Roman legionaries – so that it was indeed in Roman terms 'a glorious victory' – has to be put a more cynical picture. It has been pointed out with truth that the southern tribes, notably the ever friendly, ever powerful King Cogidubnus and his Atrebates of Silchester, showed no signs of joining in the fun with their more northerly fellow tribesmen and women.[18] If some disaffected Brigantes probably rallied to Boudica's side, her fellow Queen Cartimandua certainly did not: hence the grateful support the latter would receive from Rome at the time of her own tribulations around AD 70.

On the military level, it is perfectly true, as Suetonius was made to point out by Dio in his speech, that the Britons never had to besiege a city which was actually defended properly by the Romans, since Camulodunum's defences were pitiful, and Londinium's non-existent. Their defeat of Petilius was due to the success of the ambush: when the experienced Roman legionaries lured the wild Britons into their trap, they were able to cut them down without much difficulty.

And yet this is a part of the story . . . the force of a patriotic flash flood (as Boudica's rebellion is most plausibly seen) should never be underestimated. If positive hindsight, the explaining of why what did happen absolutely had to happen, is one enjoyable historical occupation, then the negative rather more dream-like dwelling on the what-might-have-been is another. Personalities come into play. The Procurator Catus Decianus fled from Londinium at the news of the fall of Camulodunum; Petilius' recklessness led to his vanquishing; it would also have been perfectly possible for Suetonius to flee from Glevum (Gloucester) and reach the continent if things had turned out differently or if he had been of a different nature. As to Queen Boudica's tactics and the potency of surprise, it was Mao Tse-tung in his brilliant and demonstrably effective essay on guerrilla warfare who advocated seizing the initiative whenever possible so that a small band of poorly equipped guerrillas could cause havoc and defeat a well-equipped army.[19]

The more victories the Britons clocked up, the more allies among their fellow tribesmen they would have gained. It was the winning side which was seductive to those with an eye to a profitable future. The Roman rule in Britain in AD 60, seventeen years after the invasion, was clearly neither so extensive nor so settled as it was afterwards to become; the memory of the people concerned is an important element where any occupation is being considered, an element not always sufficiently regarded. Many of the Britons in AD 60 – certainly Queen Boudica herself – could remember a time before the Romans came, and before the Romans ruled, and being blissfully unaware of the 'historical inevitability' of the four hundred years of Roman occupation, may have genuinely believed that they could enjoy freedom in the future.

What kind of freedom was envisaged? The answer to that question surely lies in the Roman maladministration which provoked the Iceni in the long term, as the Roman maltreatment of the Queen and her daughters provoked them in the short. The indignation of the native inhabitants of Camulodunum, compelled to labour and pay for an imperial cult, an imperial temple, alien to their religion and to their way of life, falls into the same category. It was as a patriot – of the Iceni cause – and a partisan that Queen Boudica rose. It is as a challenge to the Roman might by tribes generally termed inferior – 'nothing to fear from the Britons who are too weak to cross the sea and assault us', Strabo had written in an age before the invasion – that her uprising is best seen.

Had Queen Boudica continued her rout, challenged the army of Suetonius at a place of her own choosing – with her numbers and her desperate courage – she might have presented the picture of the winning side to the other tribal leaders. The 'glorious victory' might just conceivably have gone the other way. But this is to make her a prudent calculating Roman leader as Suetonius was. She remained and remains a Celt, bold, inspiring, but not, so far as we know, calculating.

And in this manner her story ends. Or so it must have seemed to those who knew her, with the enforced 'pacification' of the Iceni by just that fire and sword which Boudica herself had temporarily and bloodily employed. But Boudica's story did not end there. The death of this obscure British queen, buried in an unknown grave, was in fact only the beginning of the story. The phoenix Boadicea would rise from the ashes of Boudica. What happened to this phoenix later, why Boudica/Boadicea did not rest forever forgotten, is one theme of the rest of this book. The other interwoven theme is the multiple fascination exercised by the Warrior Queen, illustrated in so many different civilizations, including those where the Roman writ never ran and where the name of Boadicea was never known, each story contributing to the mosaic.

The first story – that of Zenobia – is however given as a dramatic coda to that of Boudica, because she too in her time challenged the might of Rome.

CHAPTER EIGHT

O Zenobia!

~

How, O Zenobia, hast thou dared to insult Roman emperors?

AURELIAN to Zenobia, Queen of Palmyra

The story of Zenobia, third-century Queen of Palmyra, another adversary of Rome, provides not only a dramatic coda to the story of Boudica, first-century Queen of the Iceni but also, at first sight, a peculiarly appropriate one. There are so many interesting parallels to be discovered between their respective experiences quite apart from the simple fact that Zenobia, like Boudica, led her people to war. Both women were widows when they assumed power, both women ruled in theory as regents for their offspring, both women had been married to client-rulers of Rome, both women led revolts (that is, from the Roman point of view) destined to upset an existing relationship with Rome which had apparently been comfortably established under their late husbands' sway.

Of course the status of widowhood is far from being peculiar to Boudica and Zenobia in the consideration of historic Warrior Queens. The frequent recurrence of what has been termed earlier the Appendage Syndrome – the Warrior Queen seen as an extension or prolongation of the rule of a particular great man – has produced widows as well as daughters. The nineteenth-century Rani of Jhansi is another prominent example of widowhood, as Queen Tamara of Georgia, Queen Elizabeth I of England and Indira Gandhi represent daughterhood. In her own way, the Rani of Jhansi comes close to fulfilling those conditions observed above concerning Boudica and Zenobia; not only was she a widow and a would-be regent, but she duly challenged an imperial power, except that the power in question was British not Roman.

For all these overall similarities linking the Warrior Queens of many different ages, at first inspection the Roman connection does seem to constitute a special link between Boudica and Zenobia. Once again some two hundred years after the death of Boudica, a Roman general found himself 'waging a war with a woman'. This was the accusation made against Aurelian by his fellow Romans, leaving him to expostulate in reply: 'As if Zenobia alone and with her own forces only were fighting against me . . . as a matter of fact, there is a great force of the enemy . . .' Here is another familiar syndrome at work, that of Shame, the one which caused the Romans to bow their heads in dismay after the destruction of Camulodunum, for, in the words of Dio Cassius quoted earlier, 'all this ruin was brought upon [them] . . . by a woman'.[1]

It is only the cooler light of second inspection which uncovers important differences between the two queens, both as they behaved and as they were treated. These differences serve as a salutary reminder, just before the 'real' Boudica is abandoned for the legendary Boadicea, that a host of very diverse women throughout history have fought beneath the generalized banner of 'Warrior Queen'. The similarities are often imposed from outside by the existence of the stereotype. Where the stories are undoubtedly superficially alike, as with Boudica and Zenobia, one should be careful not to ignore the dissimilarities, to enable the individual female character to struggle out from beneath the web of legend – in the case of Zenobia a rare character indeed.

Zenobia was an Arab. That is to say, inscriptions give her the full names of Septimia Zenobia in Latin or Bat Zabbai in Aramaic. Her father may have been called Zabbai (although 'Bat Zabbai' can also mean 'daughter of a merchant' in Aramaic). At all events this father was probably a native of Palmyra or Tadmor, to give the city its historic name (the exact etymology of these two names, respectively Greek and Aramaic, remains obscure). He would have been part of the proud, cultured and wealthy

Arab merchant-aristocracy who inhabited this splendid city, half religious monument, half commercial centre, situated at a vital confluence of caravan routes in the Syrian desert.[2]

If Zenobia's descent was predominantly Palmyrene Arab, she may well have had dashes of many other bloods including Aramaean. She flourished after all in that interesting Middle Eastern area, the world's ancient crucible, where the three languages Greek, Latin and Aramaic, in which Palmyrene inscriptions are expressed, stand for a confluence of cultures and races as well as trade routes. Some Jewish blood has been suggested on the ground that she treated the Jews of Alexandria sympathetically; but this was in fact a comprehensible political move, the Jews always forming a potential anti-Roman force since Titus' destruction of all Jerusalem in AD 70. (Individuals who treat a given Jewish community with sympathy are often supposed to be of Jewish descent: a commentary on the long history of the Jews as a persecuted people.) But it is significant that Zenobia, who made much of historic bonds, never claimed one with Solomon, which in view of his mythic connection to the fortress of Tadmor would seem to dispose of a real Jewish link.[3]

The great Cleopatra (herself predominantly Greek but acting out the Egyptian with verve) was as it were the role model to which Zenobia aspired. Moreover the Palmyrene Queen claimed very firmly to be descended from her; there was a certain history of Alexandria, dedicated 'to Cleopatra', of which Zenobia must have been the actual dedicatee. The claim is generally thought to be false, although Zenobia's knowledge of the Egyptian language and her predisposition towards Egyptian culture may conceivably indicate that her mother was Egyptian.[4] The real significance of the claim is as a proof of Zenobia's intelligence: she quickly appreciated the self-aggrandizement to be derived from a glamorous historic connection. As Cleopatra used the image of the goddess Isis, the Queen of War, to lend exciting credence to her own dreams of empire, so Zenobia drew Cleopatra's own image to her. She also incidentally associated herself with Semiramis, and loved to dress up 'in the robes of Dido':[5] one has the impression that no queen, however unfortunate her history, was left unturned in Zenobia's relentless (but practical) evocation of female majesty.

Zenobia's fantasies about Egypt should not be allowed to obscure the strong tradition to which she actually belongs. Zenobia is in fact part of a discernible pattern of pre-Islamic Arabian queens with military connections, many of them coming from her own Syrian homeland or areas adjacent. The researches of Nabia Abbott have revealed at least two dozen of these formidable ladies over six centuries, following the visit of the Queen of Sheba to Solomon in the tenth century BC. Various origins have been ascribed to this fabulous Queen including south Arabian and Abyssinian: more importantly she exemplifies 'the exercise of the right of independent queenship among the ancient Arabs'.[6]

The Assyrian records give glimpses of troublesome Arab queens such as Zabibi, finally subjugated and forced to pay tribute in 738 BC, and Samsi, who may have been her successor and, after military defeat, underwent the same fate. It was from the royal house of Emesa, annexed to Syria, that the Emperor Septimius Severus in about AD 185 chose as his wife Martha, the daughter of the priest–king – she who became the powerful Julia Domna and introduced the Semitic goddess Tanit (as Caelestis Dea) to the Roman world. Mamaea, the redoubtable daughter of Julia Domna's sister, Julia Maesa, ruled for her son the Emperor Alexander, even accompanying him on the German campaign in 234; a generation older than Zenobia, but hailing from the same 'Syrian' cradle, she was described by Gibbon as having 'manly ambition'.[7]

Nor did this tradition end with Zenobia herself: from about AD 373 to 380, a hundred years after Zenobia's disappearance from the scene of history, we encounter another Syrian Arab queen named Mawia, probably a Ghassanid. Mawia too rode in person at the head of her army, made excursions into Phoenicia and Palestine, ravaged the land to the frontiers of Egypt, and defeated the Roman armies; later she sent her fleet of Arab cavalry to the aid of the Romans when they in their turn were hard-pressed by the Goths. The last 'queen' of pre-Islamic Western Arabia was the famous – or infamous – Hind Al-Hunūd about whom many traditions have congregated, some bloodthirsty, but all pointing to her independence. And it is worth recalling too that as late as 656 Aishah, 'the beloved of Muhammad' (the Prophet's last wife), was present at the Battle of the Camels at the heart of the fighting. More than that, Aishah's role in the internecine strife of which this battle was the culmination showed that at this date men would still follow a woman to war.[8]

Zenobia may have looked to Cleopatra for inspiration, but Zenobia's Arab tradition in which, as with the Celts, queens could ride to battle (and to victory) was an important element in her story. And the Holy Figurehead element in a woman's presence at the scene of battle as an inspiration, even a quasi-goddess, was also common to the Arabs, as to the Celts, in the pre-Islamic tradition of the Lady of Victory. By this tradition, some woman of quality would be placed within the portable *qubbah* or sacred pavilion of the tribal deity and, with her attendants, form a sacred group within sight of the warriors, singing songs of encouragement to them. The Lady of Victory, her hair flowing and her body partly exposed, embodied an appeal to valour and passion. (As late as the nineteenth century, William Palgrave described one particular 'huge girl' who encouraged the Amjan Bedouins against the heir to the throne of Nejed in this manner; when she was slain, they were defeated.)[9]

Another crucial element in Zenobia's career was the geographical situation of Palmyra itself, halfway between the two mighty and contending empires, one of which was Roman. It would be equally unsuitable to regard Zenobia as some kind of Hollywood 'Desert Queen', riding out of a dust storm, with a tent for her court and a palm frond for her sceptre, as it would be to regard Boudica as a woad-stained shrieking Celtic savage. Both women – both leaders – came from complex civilizations; in the case of Zenobia, the civilization from which she sprang had been affected deeply by that of Rome.

Around AD 114, Palmyra had theoretically become part of the Roman Empire, while the Emperor Hadrian judiciously allowed the city considerable liberty in order to benefit from its celebrated archers as defenders of what was now his own frontier against the Parthians. Moreover the Palmyrenes were allowed to be responsible for their own municipal taxes: another wise move. Palmyra flourished under this loose mutually beneficial tutelage. At the beginning of the third century the Emperor Septimius Severus made Palmyra into a colony and allowed a properly elected senate to manage its affairs; distinguished Palmyrenes began to add Roman names to their Semitic ones.

As Zenobia was not an unsophisticated Bedouin queen, so Palmyra itself was not a remote and ruined city lost in the midst of sands, as some ancient geographers suggested. On the contrary, vital caravan routes linked it to the seaboard cities of Phoenicia, to Emesa, to Damascus and to Egypt itself, Palmyra providing the link between these and Seleucia, and the more distant eastern regions. Foreign armies might not easily penetrate the intervening deserts, but the camel caravans of the merchants had no such problems. So the substantial animals toiled endlessly to and fro – camels in prime condition could carry loads of up to 200 kilos – and thus the Palmyrene merchants emulated Macaulay's Lars Porsena, who 'bade his messengers ride forth, east and west and south and north, To summon his array'; except that the camels of the Palmyrenes bore back with them an array of goods, not soldiers: from perfumes and aromatic oils to skins and salt. A tariff of commercial dues dated AD 137 reveals how far afield the tentacles of Palmyrene trade actually spread: silks and jade from the Chinese frontiers are listed, and from India muslins, spice, ebony, ivory and pearls.[10]

The merchant–aristocrats lived well: in their day two emperors visited Palmyra. The merchants made great profits and patronized the arts with their money (it is always agreeable to find these two activities considered compatible). A hundred years before Zenobia, a special tax was imposed on imported bronze statues and busts; the wealthy citizens had a special penchant for erecting columns and colonnades and adorning them with self-congratulatory inscriptions. Jewellery loaded down the women – how Zenobia would one day come to feel the weight of those splendid jewels! If the colonnaded edifices showed the influence of Rome, the shadow of Palmyra's other great neighbour also fell across her culture: local deities might be given Roman names but wear Parthian dress. Later Persian costume, rugs and jewels mingled with the Roman styles.

Central to Palmyra was the great Temple of the Sun.[11] Yet by the third century the official sun worship of the Palmyrene state was being supplemented by an alternative religion: a vague yet spiritual kind of monotheism – the worship of the unknown god, to whom those inferior categories of women and servants also made offerings. Here, where the unknown god and the celestial pantheon of other gods were content to receive harmless sacrifices of incense and wine, a generally liberal atmosphere prevailed, in which, according to inscriptions, the Jews also found their place (and adapted to Palmyrene customs).

The collapse of the Parthian Empire and the arrival of the Sassanids to the newly imperial throne of Persia in AD 227 put an end to a status quo which had been prosperous and far from disagreeable for Palmyra. At the same time the worldwide vigour of imperial Rome was declining – or to be more specific the emperors were obsessed by the Gothic threat on their northern frontiers. Obviously new perils threatened what was, to outsiders, essentially the buffer state of Palmyra. It was against this background of transitional turmoil that Odainat (otherwise Septimius Odenaethus), husband of Zenobia and self-styled King of Palmyra, decided like Shakespeare's Henry v to pluck the flower of opportunity.

Zosimus, a fifth-century Greek whose history of the Roman Empire up till 410 casts an interesting light on Zenobia, refers to Odainat as a 'person whose ancestors had always been highly respected by the emperors'. Certainly Odainat came of an illustrious family. His grandfather – or possibly great-grandfather, at any rate another Odainat – had become a Roman senator in about AD 230, eighteen years after all free men within the Empire were made Roman citizens. The son or grandson of this first Odainat, Hairan (Herodianus), was the first to bear the equivocal title of chief of Palmyra – or in Aramaic Ras Tadmor.[12]

Odainat, son of Hairan and husband of Zenobia, was made a Roman consul in AD 258. Two years later the Roman Emperor Valerian was defeated by Sapor 1 of Persia, held captive in disgusting conditions and finally killed. It was under these circumstances that Odainat took to the field with the archers and spearmen of Palmyra on the one hand, the cavalry of the desert Arabs on the other; remnants of the tattered Roman legions may also have assisted him. Palmyra might have preferred to lean towards Persia rather than towards Rome, in view of the latter's debilitated state. It was the Persian Emperor who declined to lean towards Palmyra. Under the circumstances Odainat had little choice but to sally forth against him.

As it was, Odainat's forces swept all before them, and according to one chronicler they finally captured the magnificent treasure of the Persian Emperor. In 261 Odainat secured another victory at Emesa (now Homs) in western Syria, where a Roman general had taken advantage of the fluid times to set himself up as a usurper. Very likely, Odainat had been given some general title of command by Rome before he sallied forth. But in 262 the incoming Roman Emperor Gallienus – himself capable of avenging the murdered Valerian – made Odainat, the man who could actually do so, officially *dux romanorum* and later *imperator*.

There is some understandable confusion over what these titles actually meant. For one thing, they must have meant different things to the Romans, who were particular about the niceties of such things but absent, and to the Palmyrenes themselves, not so particular but on the spot. There is no evidence that Odainat was granted the distinctive title of Augustus by Gallienus or, more to the point, claimed it. He did have himself inscribed as 'King of kings' at Palmyra – but then Palmyra was a long way from Rome.[13] Odainat was a realist: he showed himself content with the substance of his power, the fact that he had saved the fortunes of the Roman Empire in the east and shored up those of Palmyra.

It was however not Odainat himself but Zenobia who mesmerized ancient historians. The so-called *Scriptores Historiae Augustae* – a collection of biographies, probably written in the fourth century, dealing with the Roman emperors from AD 117 to 284 – are full of her praises. Of the six authors to whom the *Scriptores* are attributed, 'Trebellius Pollio' and 'Flavius Vopiscus' are responsible for the period in which Zenobia flourished.[14] 'The noblest of all the women of the East', wrote Trebellius Pollio, dilating also on her personal charms: she was also *speciosissima* – 'the most beautiful' – and elsewhere *venustatis incredibilis* – 'of an incredible attraction'. His description of Zenobia – eyes black and powerful beyond the usual wont, teeth so white that many believed she wore pearls in her mouth, complexion wonderfully dark – suggests that we may look for her type among the surviving portraiture of Palmyrene art, where the impressive women with their strong noses and enormous almond-shaped eyes look out with baleful dignity; a type indeed not far from that of Zenobia's proclaimed ancestress Cleopatra.[15]

At the same time these historians, writing of course with hindsight and a full knowledge of Zenobia's remarkable career, were quick to praise her more 'masculine' qualities: her hardihood for example. Odainat himself was celebrated for his hunting; he would live in the forests and endure heat, rain and other hardships in pursuit of lions, panthers and bears: in this way he was naturally equipped for the rigours of his Persian campaigns. But Zenobia too went on these hunting trips, and so she was fit enough to accompany him on his military sorties.

Not only was she fit enough – disdaining the comfort of a woman's coach and even a man's chariot, in favour of a horse – but she was also sufficiently daring. Zosimus considered flatteringly enough that Zenobia had 'the courage of a man; and with the assistance of her husband's friends, acted in every respect as well as he had done'. But Trebellius Pollio went much further. When he wrote that Zenobia 'in the opinion of many was held to be *more* brave than her husband', he was expressing an opinion, often linked to the Shame Syndrome, but also a syndrome in its own right, which makes the woman 'the better man of the two'. There is no real reason to suppose that Zenobia was more courageous than Odainat, who sounds to have been both a vigorous general and a brave soldier; she was undeniably more reckless. It was Zenobia's gender which gave her the advantage. Because of that, even to parallel the achievements of her husband inexorably made Zenobia the Better-Man.

In other ways the idealized portrait of Zenobia as a Warrior Queen neatly encompasses the most useful qualities of both sexes. Her voice, as has been mentioned apropos that of Boudica, was not harsh (unfeminine) but clear and manly (useful for rallying the troops). Leaping off her horse, she could walk with her footsoldiers three or four miles. Indeed, Zenobia had little taste for having other women about her, eunuchs being preferred to maidservants. She could also drink-with-the-boys (like the voice, the question of drinking-with-the-boys being another perennial if unstressed problem for female rulers). But her chroniclers emphasized that Zenobia never drank without an ulterior motive: either she drank diplomatically with foreigners such as the Persians in order to get them drunk; or she drank graciously with her own generals. Either way, this rare creature was, it seems, never by any chance intoxicated.

Then there is the bizarre matter of Zenobia's famous 'chastity'. The exact number, order of birth and indeed names of Zenobia's various sons are not clear. What is quite certain is that she gave birth to at least three and possibly more. Marital relations with Odainat therefore could hardly be denied. But by a brilliant piece of propaganda, Zenobia's undoubted periodic admission of Adainat to the marriage bed was transformed into actual evidence of her chastity: 'she would not know even her own husband, except for the purpose of conception', wrote Trebellius Pollio. 'For when once she had lain with him, she would refrain until the time of the month to see if she was pregnant; if not, she would again grant an opportunity of begetting children.'

Zenobia's semi-Lysistratan policy was to gain her the awed respect of subsequent (male) historians, as it impressed the fourth-century Trebellius Pollio. Gibbon allowed Zenobia to surpass Cleopatra in both '*chastity* and valour' and one cannot help thinking that her reputation for the former subtly helped on her reputation for the latter. 'How praiseworthy was this decision in a woman!' wrote Boccaccio, describing Zenobia as 'so virtuous . . . that she must precede all other foreign women in fame'. He then indulged in a wonderful fantasy concerning her tomboy girlhood. Boccaccio has Zenobia scorning womanly exercises and wandering the forests instead to kill goats and stags with her arrows. She also wrestles with young men, carefully preserving her virginity at all points, in the passage – strongly reminiscent of Virgil on the subject of Camilla of the Volscians – cited earlier. As a grown woman, Boccaccio's Zenobia hides her beauty under armour, and never speaks to her soldiers except behind the protection of her helmet, a detail captured by Ben Jonson in his *Masque of Queenes* of 1610, whose illustration shows Zenobia 'the chaste' in her 'cask' or helmet but with long curling hair flowing beneath it, to say nothing of one exposed breast, liable, one would think, to inflame the least wanton soldier.[16]

Naturally the truth of the legend concerning Zenobia's 'chastity' can hardly be established at this point. A sceptic might be forgiven for requiring further evidence that this alluring wife of an Eastern potentate actually carried out her stringent method of sex control. But that is less important in the context than the excitement which the legend of the husband-denying Zenobia produces. The Chaste Syndrome accords well with a satisfyingly puritanical picture of the warrior-woman, the pure figurehead, her holy virginity equated with the holiness of her cause. By throwing in the theory of sex control, even married women like Zenobia can belong to it.

Around AD 266 or 267 the problem of marital attentions, if it existed, ceased to trouble Zenobia altogether. Under circumstances which have never been fully unravelled, her husband Odainat met his death. The ostensible assassin was his nephew Maeonius, whom Odainat had punished for insubordination. In the same attack also died Odainat's presumed heir, Hairan; this was the son of his first marriage, the typically unsatisfactory offspring of a successful general, being given to 'Grecian luxury'. That left Zenobia, the second wife, to assume the regency of Palmyra on behalf of her own son Vaballathus Athenodorus.

Any stepmother who sees an elder son preferred by right of birth to her own, and then lives to witness her own offspring benefiting from this son's premature death, stands to be suspected of complicity in the crime.[17] If Zenobia did help Hairan on his way, she was certainly not the first stepmother to do so. The hard evidence against Zenobia does not seem to go further than this *post hoc, propter hos* kind of argument, nor does the ambitious temperament she subsequently revealed necessarily make her a murderess even if matters had indubitably turned out conveniently for her. Zenobia however is far from being the only person who had something to gain from the death of Odainat. There is also the question of Rome.

Although the Romans appeared to acquiesce in Odainat's tacit assumption of viceregal powers, they had plenty of historical experience of self-styled emperors-in-the-East, none of it satisfactory. The perennial problem was how to secure their frontiers and yet keep down their various mushrooming lieutenants. It may be that the removal of Odainat, that hardy and effective general, was not displeasing to them; it may even be that they conspired to secure it. A youngish woman as regent for a boy would present much less of a threat. Or so the Romans thought.

As it was, Zenobia's immediate reaction to her new position was more that of the swift voracious hawk than that of the placid domestic dove. Swiftly she struck against Egypt, taking advantage of the fact that the Roman Empire itself was being hard-pressed on its other frontiers, notably in northern Italy, by those unwelcome strangers at the European feast, the Goths. (Their first attacks had occurred about thirty years earlier.) By 269 her general Zabdas had secured most of the country; at the same time Zenobia had simply annexed most of Syria to the Palmyrene kingdom. Some local difficulties with Egypt – where many distinctly preferred the distant Roman overlordship to that of neighbouring Palmyra – meant a second campaign by Zabdas. But in neither case – Egypt or Syria – was the beleaguered Roman Emperor Gallienus in any position to protest.

It was then the turn of Asia Minor: by 270 Zenobia had conquered as far as Bithynia, which commanded the Bosphorus. Only at Chalcedon were the gates closed against the Palmyrenes, who, far from their base, could not take the city. Nevertheless in the few years since her husband's death, Zenobia, in a great swathe of conquest, had sickled out a vast new empire for the tiny Palmyrene state from Egypt in the south right up to the Bosphorus in the north. And to crown it all Zenobia now took a step which Odainat had never taken: she declared herself formally independent of Rome.

By this time, Zenobia was controlling not only much of the commerce so vital to Rome – which depended for example on Egypt entirely for corn supplies – but also the trade routes with Abyssinia, Arabia and India. In addition, her northern swathe brought her in touch with the Bosphoran route to Thrace. Yet despite the menace of this eastern situation, the Roman Emperor still preferred – however grudgingly – to allow some form of concordat with Zenobia, while the still greater Gothic threat remained to be eliminated. In the words of the *Scriptores Historiae Augustae* on the fortunes of Rome at this point: 'Now all shame is exhausted, for in the weakened state of the commonwealth . . . even women ruled most excellently.'[18]

Whether Zenobia ruled excellently or not, depending on one's view of extended conquest, she certainly ruled, and with a deliberate pomp which pointed most magisterially back towards that of Cleopatra; even the gold vessels used at her banquet were said to have been those bequeathed by the great Queen. Furthermore Zenobia established a court known, however briefly, for its intellectual brilliance as well as the more material coruscation of its jewellery. Prominent among the scholars and men of letters who surrounded her at her invitation was Cassius Longinus, the eminent writer on Greek rhetoric and philosophy, himself probably Syrian. Then there was Callinicus Sutorius, originally from Petra, a sophist and historian who had taught at Athens. It was Callinicus who actually wrote that history of Alexandria – significantly, capital of the Ptolemies – which was sometimes ascribed to Zenobia herself. But then the desire, however wistful, to be known as a published scholar is not in itself an ignoble ambition for a prince – or a princess. Moreover Zenobia's was an empire founded on tolerance rather than exclusivity. Her benevolence towards the Jews of Alexandria has been mentioned. According to tradition, she also established relations with Paul of Samosata, the Christian Bishop of Antioch, condemned for certain doctrinal errors at the Synod of Antioch held in 268.[19]

What was the mainspring of all this imperial – and imperious – activity on the part of the Palmyrene Queen? The recreation of vanished Ptolemaic glories was a thrilling pursuit indeed, yet it was a chimera, one which had never haunted the more hard-headed and practical Odainat. With Zenobia, acting on behalf of her son Vaballathus, on the other hand, one can trace the mounting tenor of her claims through various inscriptions in Egypt, Syria and Palmyra, as the break with Rome gets nearer. Vaballathus was not only *dux romanorum* like his father, but *rex* and *basileus* (Greek for king) and despot – ruler. Zenobia herself was *regina* and *basilissa* – queen – and, most magnificently, the two of them were Augustus and Augusta. Finally, at some date after 11 March 271 and before August, Zenobia on behalf of Vaballathus struck money in both their names.[20] This was a declaration of war against the Empire.

The French authority on the history and customs of Palmyra, J. G. Février, knew the answer to Zenobia's driving force. For the impartial historian, he wrote, one trait dominates her character: '*une ambition féroce, insatiable*'.[21] One may be far more partial

towards Zenobia, sympathetic to the problems which she over-
came and to the near-miraculous achievements which for
however short a span were hers, and still find the answer to be
the right one. How else could she have urged her troops on that
extraordinary sweep of conquest, how else set up her Cleopatrine
court, if she had not been animated by ferocious and certainly
insatiable ambition? This is where Zenobia, as a type of Warrior
Queen, parts company significantly with Boudica, and with many
others of the Boadicean ilk, who for one reason and another were
driven into a military solution.

Unlike Boudica, Zenobia had not been wronged: she had not
been scourged, her daughters had not been raped, the Romans
had not taken over her people's land nor imposed lethal taxes
upon Palmyra. Following the pattern of Odainat, there was an
opportunity here for renewed Palmyrene aggrandizement while
the Empire remained weak, even if the Palmyrene archers, no
longer supplemented by Roman legionaries, would have to look
out for the Persian enemy on their other frontier. But Zenobia –
in this indeed like Cleopatra – preferred a bolder course.

It is not clear whether Zenobia ever claimed formal joint rule
with her own son[22] and since she enjoyed effective power during
Vaballathus' youth one can only imagine how she would have
dealt with the problem of his majority had the Palmyrene Empire
survived so long. As it was, her style of majesty, like the
Palmyrene culture to which she belonged, took profitably from
the worlds which she straddled. Symbolically, the vast oriental
jewel which hung from her helmet was not the kind of brooch
generally worn by women, but that of Eastern kings, for Zenobia
copied the regal pomp of the Persians in her banquets and the
obeisance she received; on the other hand she stepped forth to
public assemblies like the Roman emperors. Zenobia was the
type of striking and intelligent woman whose original Appendage
status is soon forgotten. When the enveloping masculine
carapace was broken, she stepped out from the fragments of the
shell with zest.

*

Zenobia was not to be allowed to pursue her daring course with impunity for ever. It is generally and plausibly believed that the new Roman Emperor Aurelian took the initiative in what followed. The time was at last propitious. Aurelian, a general who probably originally came from Lower Moesia, had done well in northern Italy against the invading Alemanni and Juthungi. The Dalmatian invasions were for the time being held off, and at home a revolt in the Senate had been quashed. Nor could Palmyra look towards Persia for any assistance against the traditional Roman enemy: it was now the turn of that empire to be paralysed by inner troubles following the death of Sapor 1. Even if Zenobia provoked the actual outbreak of hostilities by cutting off the vital supply of Egyptian corn to Italy, she could not have expected her joyous suzerainty over such a vast area – all of it contiguous to the Roman overlordship – to remain unchallenged for long once Rome itself had the energy to spare.

Aurelian's first task was to secure the reconquest of Egypt, under the generalship of Probus. This was not a task which presented too many difficulties since the Palmyrene presence was still the cause of much Egyptian resentment. At a conference at Palmyra itself, on the other hand, in August 271, a bare year since Zenobia's bold essay of independence, pledges of loyalty were given to the family of Odainat, in effect to the Queen.

Two oracles were now consulted by the Palmyrenes concerning the fate of their eastern empire: the Apollo Sarpedonius at Seleucia and the Venus Aphacitis (of Aphaca in Syria). On a grander scale, it was a situation reminiscent of Boudica's rally when she first invoked the goddess Andraste and then released the hare from the folds of her skirt 'as a species of divination'. But the hare – doubtless by careful stage management – had run off in an auspicious direction. The Apollo Sarpedonius returned an answer which indicated that he found the mere enquiry odious:

> Accursed race! Avoid my sacred fane
> Whose treach'rous deeds the angry gods disdain.[23]

As for the Venus Aphacitis, she declined to instigate that phenomenon of a rounded airy figure, appearing from a lamp of fire, which sometimes greeted the fortunate; and the Palmyrene offerings at her cistern floated unhappily on the surface, a sign that the goddess had rejected them.

As things turned out, Boudica's auspiciously lolloping hare proved to be a false prophet, whereas the Apollo Sarpedonius and the Venus Aphacitis could have claimed the satisfaction, in some pantheon where they had gloomy colloquy with each other, of getting things absolutely right. But then what omen, favourable or otherwise, has ever altered the course of history? The fact was that with a strong Roman presence back on the Eastern scene, the luck of Zenobia – and Palmyra – was fast running out.

Aurelian's first campaign took him as far as Ankara. The city duly opened its gates since the Palmyrenes had not left behind a garrison, either because Ankara was judged too far from their centre of operations, or because they had insufficient troops to do so. The first resistance encountered by Aurelian was in the defiles of Taurus, commanded by the city of Tyana, which the Palmyrenes held. Possibly aided by treachery, Aurelian was able to prevail. But he did not permit his troops to sate themselves on pillage in the customary manner – yet. After all, as he pointed out, resplendent and wealthy Palmyra lay ahead.

The Palmyrenes fell back on the line of the Orontes river, which flows north-west from Emesa to Antioch. Here just outside Antioch the two armies faced each other: but it was far from being such a disparate confrontation as that of Romans and Britons at Boudica's 'last battle'. It is true that the Roman legions were once again veterans of a life of war, such as those Suetonius had had at his command; Aurelian also had some light cavalry. But he had no archers or heavy cavalry. The Palmyrenes on the other hand had both: and the prowess of their archers was renowned throughout the East. Zenobia's line of battle consisted of a line of archers on foot, with an imposing mass of both cavalry and infantry behind; unfortunately her cavalry, famous too for its zest and power, had a tendency to lose touch with the infantry due to the unchecked depth of its charge.

In the battle which followed, with Zenobia seen galloping alongside her troops although transmitting orders through her general Zadbas, this lack in restraint on the part of the Palmyrene cavalry proved crucial. Zosimus tells us that the Romans pretended to flee, luring the Palmyrenes on until both men and horses were 'thoroughly tired, through the excessive heat and weight of their armour'.[24] As a result the Palmyrene cavalry was cut off and subjected to the most frightful slaughter.

Following this reverse, it even took a trick on the part of Zabdas to secure his re-entry to Antioch (he pretended to be leading in the captive Aurelian) since the waning fortunes of the Palmyrenes were evident to their subjugated neighbours. Zenobia, pursued by Aurelian, now fell back on Emesa, and it was here, on the banks of the Orontes, some five or six miles north of modern Homs, that her 'last battle' took place. According to Zosimus, Zenobia at this point still had, out of those Syrians loyal to her, seventy thousand men. But Aurelian's own troops, augmented by reinforcement, may by this stage have been almost as numerous.

The battle was long and fierce: but in the end the fiery Palmyrenes, for all their archers and their cavalry, were no more match for the seasoned Roman legionaries than the warriors of the Iceni had been, with their decorated shields, chariots and long swords. The Roman staying-power could not be gainsaid. Once again the Palmyrene cavalry failed to re-form after its initial charge, and the Emperor was able to throw in his footsoldiers against them. 'The slaughter was promiscuous,' wrote Zosimus, 'some falling by the sword and others by their own and their enemies' horses.'[25] The field was covered with dead men and animals. So fell the flower of the Palmyrene aristocracy.

But Zenobia did not fall. After a grim council of war, the decision was taken to abandon Emesa for the base stronghold of Palmyra, where at least the Palmyrenes would not have to contend with growing Syrian hostility. Zenobia's withdrawal across the desert to Palmyra – a distance of perhaps one hundred miles – was something to which custom had habituated both her and her Arab troops. Aurelian's pursuit, given the terrain and the ability of the nomads who inhabited it to harry him, was more of an ordeal and thus more of an achievement. And, once he had arrived to set up his blockade, Palmyra's isolated position, with the caravans no longer active, told against her rather than her enemies. In the subsequent siege, it was famine as much as anything else which ravaged the inhabitants.

Zenobia however had not lost her spirit. It was at this point that her chronicler has her engaging in a correspondence with Aurelian on the subject of surrender.[26] Aurelian was already publicly bemoaning his fate in being matched against a woman in that passage quoted earlier: 'as if Zenobia was contending against me with her own strength alone . . .' To the Queen herself he wrote in contemptuous terms: 'And you, O Zenobia, may pass your life in some spot where I shall place you in pursuance of the distinguished sentence of the Senate; your gems, your silver, gold, silk, horses, camels, being given up to the Roman treasury.'

'Thou askest me to surrender', replied the Palmyrene Queen proudly, 'as if thou wert ignorant that Queen Cleopatra chose rather to perish than to survive her dignity.' In answer to Aurelian's indignant question: 'How, O Zenobia, hast thou dared to insult Roman emperors?' she answered: 'Thee I acknowledge to be Emperor, since thou has conquered', but the rest of them, including Gallienus, she did not consider worthy of the name of chief – *princeps*. She added: 'Believing Vitruvia* to be a woman like me, I desired to become a partner in the royal power, should the supply of lands permit.'

At the same time as firing off this defiant letter – about the authorship of which there would later be some significant dispute – Zenobia sought assistance from the Persians. It is kindest and

---

* Victoria or Vitruvia, the influential mother of the rebel Gallic Emperor Victorinus (who succeeded Postumus in 268/9); she also helped the next Gallic Emperor, Tetricus, to power.[27]

by no means unreasonable to regard Zenobia's subsequent secret flight from Palmyra as part of her plan for securing this Persian help, since Aurelian blocked off not only supplies but also any overt Persian relief force. Taking a female camel – 'which is the swiftest of that kind of animal, and much more swift than horses' – she managed to slip out of the beleaguered city. Riding furiously, Zenobia got as far as the Euphrates. Here she was captured as she was boarding a boat, either recognized or betrayed. Taken to Emesa, Zenobia found herself once more facing the Emperor Aurelian, but this time unaided by Palmyrene archers or cavalry.

Palmyra itself was captured and sacked. But in the persons of Aurelian and Zenobia an interesting battle of the sexes was joined, one from which the Palmyrene Queen undoubtedly emerged victorious. Aurelian for his part remained uneasy at his triumph over a mere woman, and reflected that in ages to come it might not redound entirely to his credit to have done so. He therefore continued to stress at length the amazing qualities of the Palmyrene Queen: a woman perhaps, but what a woman! So brave, bold, daring, prudent in council, firm in purpose, etc., etc. Moreover Odainat's victories in Persia were due entirely to her, 'such was the dread entertained of this woman, among the natives of the East and of Egypt, that she kept in check the Arabians, the Saracens and the Armenians'.[28] Frantically Aurelian attempted to elude the taint of the Shame Syndrome, generally supplied to those who were actually defeated by 'mere women' like Boudica, but still capable of adhering to those who defeated them.

Zenobia on the other hand, displayed an impudence which should make her the admiration of any strong-minded woman finding herself in a tight corner in a masculine-oriented society. She simply turned round and claimed immunity on the grounds of her sex. In short, she 'produced many persons, who had seduced her as a simple woman'. Even her bold letter of defiance to Aurelian was now ascribed to the scholar Longinus, although another scholar Nicomachus asserted to the contrary that Zenobia had dictated the letter to him personally, in order that he should translate it into Greek (which she could speak but not write).[29] As a result, Longinus was executed. Zenobia however survived, as presumably had been her intention: for nothing more was heard after this of her bold desire to 'perish rather than lose her dignity'.

All the evidence points to the fact that Zenobia was now taken captive to Rome. Zosimus is the only dissenting voice, but then in suggesting that Zenobia died on her way to Europe by her own hand he was manifestly trying to emphasize the identity of Zenobia with Cleopatra. Other versions agree with a wealth of circumstantial detail that Zenobia reached Italy in safety where she was obliged to walk in the Emperor's triumph.[30]

One would like to have witnessed this apotheosis of the Emperor Aurelian, although preferably not in chains. First came a parade of the most curious wild beasts, including not only elephants but tigers, giraffes and elks: subsequently the prudent Aurelian gave this menagerie to various Roman citizens so that the privy purse would not be burdened with their upkeep. Then came the gladiators and then the ambassadors of such diverse empires as Ethiopia, Persia, India and China. The human menagerie which followed was of no less interest to the inquisitive spectators: captives from, as it seemed, every corner of the globe attesting to the range of Aurelian's victories, and all neatly labelled with placards round their necks to din in the geography lesson (as diplomats today are labelled at a United Nations session). In this manner there trailed past not only the recent victims of the East, but also Hibernians, Vandals, Franks and Swabians. Among these last were a group of Gothic women who had been discovered fighting in men's clothes: helpfully the placards around their necks read 'Amazon'.

Four chariots in all formed part of the procession. One of these, which had once belonged to the King of the Goths, was drawn by stags: at the Capitol the stags would be slain and vowed to the altar of Jupiter. The others were of Eastern provenance: the chariot of Odainat, adorned with silver and gold, the chariot given to Aurelian by the Emperor of Persia, and the chariot of

Zenobia (that chariot in which she had often disdained to ride, preferring with her 'masculine energy' the hardihood of horse-back).

It was indeed Zenobia herself, walking in front of her chariot, who was the focus of every eye. She bore no placard round her neck, nor was she labelled 'Amazon' or for that matter 'Penthesilea' or 'Hippolyta'. Nevertheless the half-fainting Palmyrene Queen (for once she might have been glad of that chariot), shackled by golden fetters and weighed down by the very mass of those jewels she had once displayed so proudly, stood by her very presence for Aurelian's victory in the East, much as the Greek heroes' legendary victories over the Amazons had symbolized the victory of Greeks over the barbarians.

Zenobia, the great survivor, survived the ordeal of the Triumph. She did more than that: she built a new life.[31] At some later point, she seems to have married a Roman senator. At any rate she was able to retire in affluence to a villa, granted to her by the Roman state, at Tibur (Tivoli), near that of Hadrian. A hundred years later her descendants, either by this second husband or by Odainat – Vaballathus disappears from view, but two other sons walked with her in the Triumph – were known in senatorial circles; the fifth-century Bishop of Florence, Zenobius, may have owed his unusual name to a still remembered ancestress.

Zenobia's instinct for survival, unlike her forcible marital chastity, has received a bad press from historians, although one can detect a certain gloomy satisfaction at finding a woman, however bold on the field, choosing to behave really badly in a genuine crisis. Theodor Mommsen thundered: 'Zenobia, after she had for years born rule with masculine energy, did not now disdain to invoke a woman's privileges and to throw the responsibility on her advisers.' Gibbon was more philosophical: 'as female fortitude is commonly artificial, so it is seldom steady or consistent'.[32] For tradition has it that Zenobia, unruffled by such considerations, had the bad taste to enjoy her life as a Roman matron. She held a fashionable salon in her villa, where only her outlandish Roman accent (but then she did speak Greek,

Aramaic and Egyptian) betrayed her exotic origins. As Zenobia dispensed hospitality and perhaps told stories of her tribulations walking in the Triumph or even tales of desert rides – did she ever dream of that female camel, the swiftest in the business? – Aurelian was obliged to return to Palmyra. There he quelled another insurrection. Finally both Palmyra and Alexandria were plundered to excess and the Palmyrene civilization passed away.

So finally the story of Zenobia and the Romans, as a coda to that of Boudica, reminds one that there could be advantages in being a Warrior Queen – as opposed to a Warrior King – as well as disadvantages; or at least so far as the queen herself was concerned. Boudica was scourged (and her daughters raped), which it has been suggested was a deliberate outrage on the part of the Romans, connected to Boudica's sex; Zenobia on the other hand betrayed Longinus with impunity, if one leaves out of account her short bejewelled travail on foot. The Only-a-Weak-Woman Syndrome – 'I am as good as (or even better than) a man when I ride to victory but I'm Only-a-Weak-Woman when I'm defeated' – is also part of the history of the Warrior Queen.

None of this should detract from the achievements of Zenobia in her prime. There is a figure of Arab legend called variously Zebbâ, al-Zabbà or az-Zabbà: a beautiful warrior who leads her troops to victory in a series of confrontations, as well as indulging in some wily tricks, based on her own charms.[33] Zebbâ has two fortresses on the left and right banks of the Euphrates – in some stories her sister called Zainab (the Arab version of Zenobia) occupies one of them – and in one legend at least remains chaste; moreover Zebbâ, like Zenobia, is captured in an incident at a river. Although an exact connection between Zenobia and Zebbâ cannot be made – just as a historical figure like Boudica can never be exactly connected with the legendary Boadicea – nevertheless there are too many coincidences between them to dismiss it altogether.

It therefore seems fitting, as we go forward on the long march of Boudica's mythical history, to remember that Zenobia also has her own lively myths in her own Arab culture (Zainab is a popular name in Syria today). A modern play by Assi and Mansour Al-Rahbani ends with Zenobia poisoning herself just before the Roman soldiers bind her in chains. She dies with the words 'O Liberty!' on her lips, and her mourning people promise themselves never to forget her (or the idea of liberty).[34]

It is good to bear this Arab heroine in mind; for we shall find the 'chaste' Zenobia appearing from time to time in a somewhat pallid disguise in Europe:

> That lovely form enshrines the gentlest virtues
> Softest compassion, unaffected wisdom,
> To outward beauty lending higher charms[35]

as an eighteenth-century play had it. It is difficult to imagine this 'beauteous mourner' raising her 'suppliant voice' for 'mild humanity' carving out an empire from Egypt to Asia Minor in defiance of Rome itself. 'O Zenobia, hast thou dared to insult Roman emperors?' wrote Aurelian to the real-life Queen: she had and she did. It is Zenobia's courage which links her to Boudica; her ambition (and her instinct for survival) sets her apart.

Reference Notes

～⌒～

Bibliographical details of each book or article are given at its first point of entry (the place of publication is London unless otherwise stated). Thereafter, only a short entry is given, with a note indicating where the first full reference can be found in brackets, i.e. in Chapter Four, note 6, 'Tacitus (III–1), p. 265' refers back to Chapter Three, note 1, Tacitus, *The Annals of Imperial Rome*, translated and with an Introduction by Michael Grant (revised edn 1977 pbk).

Chapter 1: A Singular Exception

'Flashes afresh . . .' is a quotation from Philip Larkin's poem 'Aubade'.

1 Research carried out at the Colindale Newspaper Library fully confirms this.

2 Jonson, Ben, *The Masque of Queenes*, with the designs of Inigo Jones (1930), p. 35.

3 Cit. Dudley, Donald R. and Webster, Graham, *The Rebellion of Boudicca* (1962), p. 130; Webster, Graham, *Boudica: The British Revolt against Rome AD 60* (1978), p. 15.

4 See Courteault, Paul, 'An Inscription Recently Found at Bordeaux', *Journal of Roman Studies*, Vol. XI (1921), pp. 102f. for a votive altar to Tutela Boudiga; Webster (1–3), p. 15.

5 Ubaldini, Petruccio, *Le vite delle Donne illustri del regno d'Inghilterra, e del regno di Scotia . . .* (1591); 'Le Vite e i Fatti de sei Donne Illustri', British Library MS 14A XIX. Translated by Angus Clarke.

6 Ogilby, John, *Africa etc . . . Collected and translated from the most authentic authors* (founded mainly on the work of O. Dapper), 2 vols (1670), Vol. II, pp. 564–5.

7 Joan Kelly's Cancer Journal, cit. Kelly, Joan, *Women, History and Theory: The Essays of Joan Kelly* (Chicago 1985), p. XV; interview with

Graham Turner, 'Feminists Count the Cost', *Sunday Telegraph*, 22 February 1987.

8 Pisan, Christine de, *The Treasure of the City of Ladies, or The Book of the Three Virtues*, translated and with an Introduction by Sarah Lawson (1985 pbk), p. 51.

9 Tocqueville, Alexis de, *Democracy in America*, 2 vols (1875), Vol. II, p. 179; Gibbon, Edward, *The History of the Decline and Fall of the Roman Empire*, edited by J. B. Bury, 7 vols, Vol. 1 (1896), p. 27.

10 E.g. Hacker, Barton C., 'Women and Military Institutions in Early Modern Europe', *Signs*, Summer 1981.

11 Cit. Abbott, Nabia, *Aishah: The Beloved of Mohammed*, Preface by Sarah Graham-Brown (1985), p. 176.

12 Gibbon (1–9), 1, p. 149.

13 De Gaulle, Charles, *The Edge of the Sword*, translated by Gerard Hopkins (1960), pp. 13–14.

14 Tacitus, *Germania*, Chs 13–14, cit. Keen, Maurice, *Chivalry* (1984), p. 55.

15 de Beauvoir, Simone, *The Second Sex* (1972 pbk); p. 21.

16 Troyat, Henri *Catherine the Great*, translated by Emily Read (1979), p. 183.

17 *A Comment on Boadicia* by W. Rider AB, late Scholar of Jesus College, Oxon (1754); Wapshott, Nicholas and Brock, George, *Thatcher* (1983 pbk), p. 240; Mrs Thatcher, by substituting the word 'failure' for 'defeat', slightly misquoted Queen Victoria.

18 Young, Hugo and Sloman, Anne, *The Thatcher Phenomenon* (BBC Publications, 1986), p. 40; Denis Healey returned to the charge in the 1987 election (13 May), calling Mrs Thatcher 'the Catherine the Great of Finchley'.

19 Boccaccio, Giovanni, *Concerning Famous Women*, translated with an Introduction by Guido A. Guarmio (1964), p. 5.

20 Campbell, Joseph, *The Masks of God: Creative Mythology* (1974), p. 519 note; Leigh Fermor, Patrick, *A Traveller's Tree: A Journey through the Caribbean Islands* (1950), p. 374.

21 Carras, Mary C., *Indira Gandhi: In the Crucible of Leadership. A Political Biography* (Bombay 1980), p. 47; Breisach, Ernst, *Caterina Sforza: A Renaissance Virago* (Chicago 1967), p. 24; cit. Duff, Nora, *Matilda of Tuscany* (1909), p. 77.

22 King, Betty, *Boadicea* (1975), p. 9.

Chapter 2: Antique Glories

1 See Ross, Anne, *Pagan Celtic Britain: Studies in Iconography and Tradition* (1967), Ch. v, pp. 204f.

2 *The Mabinogion*, translated with an Introduction by Jeffrey Gantz (1976 pbk), p. 52.

3 Ross, *Pagan* (11–1), pp. 219, 152.

4 *The Tain*, translated from the Irish epic by Thomas Kinsella (Oxford 1970 pbk), pp. 52f; I have preferred this lively unbowdlerized translation.

5 Spenser, Edmund, *The Faerie Queene*, Introduction by J. W. Hales, 2 vols (1910), Vol. I, p. 381.

6 Diner, Helen, *Mothers and Amazons* (New York 1965), p. 27.

7 Lefkowitz, Mary R., *Woman in Greek Myth* (1986), p. 177 and 'Influential Women' in *Images of Women in Antiquity*, edited by Averil Cameron and Amélie Kuhrt (1983), pp. 49–64; Pomeroy, Sarah B., *Goddesses, Whores, Wives and Slaves: Women in Classical Antiquity* (1976), p. 13 and 'A Classical Scholar's Perspective on Matriarchy' in *Liberating Women's History: Theoretical and Critical Essays*, edited by Berenice A. Carroll (Chicago 1976), pp. 217–24.

8 Todd, Malcolm, *Roman Britain 55 BC–AD 400: The Province beyond the Ocean* (1981 pbk), p. 36.

9 Sobol, Donald J., *The Amazons of Greek Mythology* (South Brunswick and New York, 1972), pp. 90ff.; Warner, Marina, *Joan of Arc: The Image of Female Heroism* (1981), Ch. x, pp. 198f.; see also Briffault, R., *The Mothers*, 3 vols (1927), Vol. II, p. 457 note 2 for a convenient list of references on this subject.

10 Lefkowitz (11–7), p. 133.

11 The *Bibliotheca Historica* of Diodorus Siculus, 2 vols (1956–7), Vol. I, pp. 199–203; Virgil, *The Aeneid*, translated into English prose by W. F. Jackson Knight (revised edn 1958 pbk), pp. 299, 200.

12 Heywood, Thomas, *Gynaekeion or Nine Books of Various History Concerning Women* (1624), p. 226.

13 Knox, John, *The First Blast of the Trumpet against the monstrous regiment of Women*, edited by Edward Arber (1880), p. 13; for the *mignons* see Davis, N. Z., *Society and Culture in Early Modern France* (1975), p. 133.

14 *Correspondence de Napoléon Ier*, Vol. XIII (Paris 1863), p. 326.

15 Kelly, Amy, *Eleanor of Aquitaine and the Four Kings* (Cambridge, Massachusetts 1950), p. 34.

16 Cit. Kelly, *Eleanor* (11–15), p. 38.

17 Green, David, *Queen Anne* (1970), p. 101.

18 Green (11–17), pp. 109, 154.

19 London *Independent*, 10 December 1986.

20 Duff (1–21), p. 274.

Chapter 3: The Queen of War

 1 Tacitus, *The Annals of Imperial Rome*, translated and with an Introduction by Michael Grant (revised edn 1977 pbk), p. 330.

 2 *Encyclopaedia Britannica* (15th edn 1974), Vol. 11, p. 983.

 3 Herodotus, *The Histories*, translated by Aubrey de Sélincourt, revised by A. R. Burn (1972 pbk), p. 115; *The Elegies of Propertius in a Reconditioned Text*, translated by S. G. Tremenheere (1932), p. 229.

 4 *The Works of Voltaire*, 22 vols (New York 1927), Vol. IX, p. 173; Diodorus Siculus (11–11), p. 153.

 5 Herodotus (111–3), pp. 123f.; Dewald, Caroline, 'Women and Culture in Herodotus' Histories', in Foley, Helene B., *Reflections of Women in Antiquity* (New York 1981), pp. 91–125.

 6 Boccaccio (1–19), p. 104.

 7 Herodotus (111–3), pp. 8, 14, 475f., 554.

 8 Moraes, Dom, *Mrs Gandhi* (1980), p. 133; George Brown, cit. *Observer*, 24 April 1988.

 9 Aylmer, John, *An Harborowe for Faithfull and Trewe Subjectes against the late blown Blast . . .* (1559).

10 Heywood (11–12), p. 204.

11 See Grant, Michael, *Cleopatra* (revised edn 1974 pbk), *passim*, which is the basis of these dates and also much of the following passage.

12 Grant (111–11), p. 37.

13 Lefkowitz (11–7), p. 57.

14 Plutarch, *Fall of the Roman Empire: Six Lives*, translated by Rex Warner (1972 pbk), p. 290.

15 Cicero, *Letters to Atticus*, translated by E. O. Winstedt, 3 vols, Vol. III (1918), pp. 337–9.

16 Cit. Grant (111–11), pp. 184–5.

17 Cit. Grant (111–11), p. 261.

18 Grant (111–11), p. 208.

19 Horace, *Odes*, translated by James Michie (1964), 1, 37, p. 87.

20 *Nine Lives by Plutarch*, Makers of Rome, translated and with an Introduction by Ian Scott-Kilvert (1972 pbk reprint), p. 280.

21 Propertius (III–3), p. 231.

22 Horace (III–19), 1, 37, p. 89; *Antony and Cleopatra*, Act v, scene ii.

23 *Dio's Roman History*, with an English translation by Earnest Cary, 9 vols, Vol. VIII (1925), pp. 83–105; Wright, F. A., *Marcus Agrippa* (1937), pp. 251–3; *Cambridge Ancient History*, Vol. x (Cambridge 1934), pp. 266–70; Macurdy, Grace H., *Vassal-Queens and Some Contemporary Women in the Roman Empire* (Baltimore 1937), p. 2.

24 Virgil (II–11), p. 173.

Chapter 4: Iceni: this Powerful Tribe

The principal sources for the following four chapters are Dudley and Webster, *The Rebellion of Boudicca* (1–3); Webster, *Boudica* (1–3); also Frere, *Britannia* (IV–15); Salway, *Roman Britain* (IV–7); and Todd, *Roman Britain* (II–8).

 1 Caesar, *De Bello Gallico*, 5, 21, in 'War Commentaries of Caesar', translated by Rex Warner (New York 1960), p. 97; Allen, D. F., 'The Coins of the Iceni', *Britannia*, Vol. 1 (1970), p. 1 note 4, writes: 'with little doubt'; but Todd (II–8), p. 24: 'Cenimagni *might* later appear as the Iceni'.

 2 Ekwall, Eilert, *Concise Oxford Dictionary of English Place-Names* (4th edn Oxford 1959), pp. 267, 268; Dudley and Webster (1–3), Appendix 11 p. 143.

 3 The famous judgement of Gibbon on Abyssinia, actually a quotation from Alexander Pope, *Eloisa to Abelard*, (1717), l, 207.

 4 Allen, 'Coins' (IV–1), p. 1.

 5 Tacitus (III–1), p. 265; Todd (II–8), p. 83 note 8.

 6 Tacitus (III–1), p. 265.

 7 Salway, Peter, *Roman Britain* (Oxford 1984 pbk), p. 101; Allen, 'Coins' (IV–1), p. 2; Todd (II–8), p. 53.

 8 See Ross, Anne, *Everyday Life of the Pagan Celts* (1970); Ross, *Pagan* (II–1); Powell, T. G. E., *The Celts* (1958), *passim*.

 9 Clarke, R. Rainbird, *East Anglia* (1960), p. 110; Piggott, Stuart, *The Druids* (1974 pbk), p. 36.

10 *The Geography of Strabo*, translated by H. L. Jones, 8 vols, Vol. II (1923), pp. 237, 247.

11 Fox, Sir Cyril, *Pattern and Purpose: A Survey of Early Celtic Art in Britain* (Cardiff 1958), p. 59 and illustration p. 58; Salway (IV–7), p. 76; Powell (IV–8), p. 109: 'no archaeological evidence' for scythed chariots.

12 Cit. Piggott (IV–9), p. 136; Clarke (IV–9), p. 99.

13 Fox (IV–11), p. 70; Allen, 'Coins' (IV–1), p. 14.

14 Allen, 'Coins' (IV–1), p. 3 and fig. 1; Tony Gregory, Norfolk Archaeological Unit, to the author, 1985.

15 Frere, Sheppard, *Britannia: A History of Roman Britain* (revised edn 1978), p. 40; Todd (II–8), p. 53; Webster (I–3), p. 24.

16 Spratling, Dr Mansel, 'Note on Santon, Norfolk, Hoard', *Britannia*, Vol. 6 (1975); Fox (IV–11), p. 84.

17 'Very heavy and uncomfortable' were the terms used to the author by one individual who tried on a torc; see Clarke, R. Rainbird, 'The Early Iron Age Treasure from Snettisham, Norfolk', *Proceedings of the Prehistoric Society* (1954); and Brailsford, John and Stapley, J. E., 'The Ipswich Torcs', *Proceedings of the Prehistoric Society* (1972).

18 Brailsford and Stapley (IV–17), p. 227; alternatively if the Snettisham torcs come from further south, the Ipswich torcs may be local.

19 Reynolds, Peter, 'Experimental Archaeology and the Butser Ancient Farm Research Project' in Collis, J., *The Iron Age in Britain* (1977), p. 37.

20 Thetford, *Current Archaeology*, no. 81 (1981), pp. 294–7; Gregory (IV–14) to author.

21 Dio (III–23), VII, p. 414–15.

22 Gardner, Jane F., *Women in Roman Law and Society* (1986), p. 5; and Balsdon, J. P. V. D., *Roman Women: Their History and Habits* (1962), *passim.*

23 Wells, Colin, *The Roman Empire* (1984 pbk), p. 271.

24 Ross, *Everyday* (IV–8), p. 146.

25 Caesar cit. Ross, *Everyday* (IV–8), p. 133; Ross, *Pagan* (II–1), pp. 62f.; Webster (I–3), p. 82.

26 Livy cit. Ross, *Everyday* (IV–8), p. 154; Strabo (IV–10), II, p. 247.

27 Tacitus (III–1), p. 266.

28 See Richmond, I. A., 'Queen Cartimandua', *Journal of Roman Studies*, Vol. 44 (1954), pp. 43–52.

29 Tacitus (III–1), p. 269.

30 Tacitus, *The Histories*, translated by Kenneth Wellesley (revised edn, 1986 pbk), p. 172; Webster, Graham, *Rome against Caractacus: The Roman Campaigns in Britain AD 48–58* (1981), p. 14.

31 Richmond (IV–28), p. 52.

32 Ubaldini, *Donne* (I–5); Milton, John, *The History of Britain . . . continu'd to the Normal Conquest* (1670), p. 60.

33 Tacitus, *The Agricola and the Germania*, translated by H. Mattingly, revised by S. A. Handford (1970 pbk), p. 66.

34 Syme, Sir Ronald, *Tacitus*, 2 vols (Oxford 1958), Vol. I, p. v.

35 Tacitus (III–1), pp. 327–32; Tacitus, *Agricola* (IV–33), pp. 65–7; Dio (III–23), VIII, pp. 83–105.

36 Syme (IV–34), I, pp. 270f.; II, p. 763.

37 Millar, Fergus, *A Study of Cassius Dio* (Oxford 1964), pp. 32f.

38 Webster (I–3), p. 105.

39 In 1962 Dudley and Webster (III–1), pp. 144f., wrote of 'a strong presumption in favour of 60 . . . with 61 not disposed of completely'; Syme (IV–34), I, p. 20 note 8 chooses 60; but in 1981 Salway (IV–7) referred to 'more recent opinion' returning to 61; i.e. Carroll, Kevin, J., 'The Date of Boudicca's Revolt', *Britannia*, Vol. x (1979), pp. 197–202, who argues for 61; however Webster (III–1) sticks to 60, as do Frere (IV–15) and Clarke (IV–9).

40 Salway (IV–7), p. 90 and note 2.

41 See Braund, David C., *Rome and the Friendly King: The Character of the Client Kingship* (1984), Part III, 'Royal Wills', p. 144 where the point is made that 'we simply do not know how Nero and the King's daughters were to divide the inheritance, for Tacitus does not tell us'.

Chapter 5: Ruin by a Woman

1 Tacitus trans. Dudley and Webster (I–3), p. 137; Tacitus, *Agricola* (IV–33), p. 66; Dio (III–23), VIII, p. 85.

2 Bulst, Christoph, 'The Revolt of Queen Boudicca in AD 60; Roman Politics and the Iceni', *Historia*, Vol. 10 (1961), p. 499.

3 Dio (III–23), VIII, p. 85; cit. Powell (IV–8), p. 76; cit. Chadwick, Nora, *The Celts* (1970), p. 50.

4 Cit. Jardine, Lisa, 'Isotta Nogarola: Women Humanists, Education for What?', *History of Education*, Vol. 12, no. 4 (1983), p. 233.

5 Donizo cit. Huddy, Mary E., *Matilda, Countess of Tuscany* (1905), p. 76; cit. Hibbert, Christopher, *The Great Mutiny, India 1857* (1978), p. 378; *The Scriptores Historiae Augustae*, with an English translation by David Magie, 3 vols (1922–32), Vol. III, p. 139; Gibbon (I–9), I, p. 302.

6 *Johnsonian Miscellanies*, ed. G. B. Hill, 2 vols (Oxford 1897), Vol. I, p. 118; Dudley and Webster (I–3), p. 46.

7 Salway (IV–7), p. 113; Braund (IV–41), p. 144.

8 Graham Webster in the *London Archaeologist*, Vol. 4, no. 15 (1984) p. 411 suggests 'Boudica and her household' may have misunderstood what was an accounting process; alternatively Catus saw an opportunity for personal gain; Tacitus (III–1), p. 328.

9 Cit. Salway (IV–7), p. 146; Brownmiller, Susan, *Against our will: Men, Women and Rape* (1975), p. 14.

10 Breisach (I–21), p. 341.

11 I.e. Salway (IV–7), p. 114.

12 Cit. Balsdon (IV–22), p. 33.

13 Dio (III–23), VIII, p. 83.

14 Salway (IV–7), p. 115.

15 See Richmond, I. A., 'The Four *Coloniae* of the Roman Empire', *Archaeological Journal*, Vol. 103 (1947), p. 57.

16 Frere (IV–15), pp. 104–5.

17 Fishwick, Duncan, 'Templum Divo Claudium Constitutum', *Britannia*, Vol. 3 (1972), pp. 168f.; Webster (I–3), p. 89.

18 See Wheeler, R. E. M. and Laver, P. G., 'Roman Colchester', *Journal of Roman Studies*, IX (1919), pp. 139–69; Crummy, Philip, 'Colchester: The Roman Fortress and the Development of the Colonia', *Britannia*, Vol. 8 (1977), pp. 65–106.

19 Dudley and Webster (I–3), p. 49.

20 Ross, *Pagan* (II–1), p. 53; also Piggott (IV–9), *passim* for the Druids.

21 Todd (II–8), p. 257; Salway (IV–7), p. 24.

22 Gibbon (I–9), I, p. 29.

23 Laing, Lloyd, *Celtic Britain* (1979), p. 81; Piggott (IV–9), p. 99; Powell (IV–8), p. 153; Ross, *Everyday* (IV–8), p. 151; Syme, Sir Ronald, *Ten Studies in Tacitus* (Oxford 1970), p. 25 and note 2.

24 Cit. Holmes, Richard, *Footsteps* (1984), p. 263.

25 Strongly argued by Webster (I–3), pp. 63f.; Richmond, I. A., *Roman Britain* (2nd edn 1963 pbk), p. 28, agrees, as does Frere (IV–15), p. 76; but see Todd (II–8), Appendix pp. 255–6 for contrary view and Dyson, Stephen L., 'Native Revolts in the Roman Empire', *History*, Vol. XX (1971), p. 260: the Druids' role has been 'exaggerated'.

26 Fox (IV–11), p. 145.

27 *Holinshed's Chronicles of England, Scotland and Ireland*, 6 vols, Vol. 1 (1807), p. 496; Milton (IV–32), p. 65; Syme (IV–34), I, p. 763 and note 6; Overbeck, John C., 'Tacitus and Dio on Boudicca's Rebellion', *American Journal of Philology*, Vol. XL (1969), p. 136 note 27.

28 See Layard, John, *The Lady and the Hare* (1944), *passim*; Ross, *Pagan* (II–I), pp. 349–50.

29 Note by Dr Anne Ross, Dudley and Webster (I–3), p. 151; Briffault (II–9), II, p. 70 note 12; Ross, *Everyday* (IV–8), p. 159; cit. Fox (IV–II), p. 139 and plate 80 no. 19.

30 Tacitus, *Histories* (IV–30), p. 247; Powell (IV–8), p. 195.

31 Dyson (V–25), p. 265.

32 Dudley and Webster (I–3), p. 57.

33 Crummy (V–18), p. 81.

34 Crummy, Philip, *Colchester, Recent Excavations and Research* (Colchester 1974).

35 Philip Crummy, Colchester Archaeological Trust, to the author, Colchester, 1985.

36 Dudley and Webster (I–3), pp. 106–7.

37 Webster (I–3), p. 117.

Chapter 6: The Red Layer

1 Todd (II–8), p. 90.

2 Tacitus, *Agricola* (IV–33), p. 63.

3 Webster (I–3), pp. 90–1.

4 See Frere, S. S. and Joseph, J. K. St., 'The Roman Fortress at Longthorpe', *Britannia*, Vol. 5 (1974).

5 Ogilvie, R. M. and Richmond, Sir Ian (eds), *Cornelii Taciti De Vita Agricolae* (Oxford 1967), p. 198 note to '*universi*'.

6 Webster (I–3), p. 90.

7 Webster (I–3), p. 93; Firth, C. H., *Cromwell's Army*, with a new Introduction by P. H. Hardacre (1967 pbk), p. 106.

8 See Merrifield, Ralph, *London: City of the Romans* (1983), pp. 41–6 and notes 1 and 2 p. 274 for a concise summary.

9 Hall, Jenny and Merrifield, Ralph, *Roman London* (HMSO 1986), p. 6.

10 Merrifield (VI–8), pp. 26–7 suggests a military origin; but see Marsden, Peter, *Roman London* (1980), pp. 22–4 for a theory of civil trading settlement.

11 Marsden (VI–10), p. 24 for acreage; Frere (IV–15), p. 296 for population, if Tacitus' figures are accepted, since his language suggests 'an official souce'.

12 Merrifield (VI–8), p. 42.

13 Marsden (VI–10), p. 26.

14 Marsden (vi–io), p. 25.

15 Webster (1–3), p. 94.

16 Dudley and Webster (1–3), p. 55.

17 See Lambert, Frank, 'Some Recent Excavations in London', *Archaeologia*, Vol. LXXI (1921), pp. 55–8; Dunning, G. C., 'Two Fires of Roman London', *Antiquaries Journal*, Vol. XXV (1945), pp. 48–50 and fig. 3.

18 Marsden (vi–io), p. 33; Report by the Police President of Hamburg, 1 December 1943, Appendix 30, *German Documents, 1943–45*, p. 311.

19 Marsden (vi–io), p. 31.

20 Merrifield (vi–8), p. 57.

21 But Marsh, Geoff and West, Barbara, 'Skulduggery in Roman London?', London and Middlesex Archaeological Society, *Transactions*, XXXII (1981) reject 'the events of AD 60' in connection with the skulls, in favour of 'Celtic religious practices connected with water'.

22 Fraser, Antonia, *Cromwell, Our Chief of Men* (1973), p. 338.

23 Tacitus, *Agricola* (IV–33), p. 66; Tacitus (III–1), p. 329; Dio (III–23), VIII, p. 95.

24 Grimal, Pierre, *The Dictionary of Classical Mythology* (1986), pp. 75–6.

25 I.e. Salway (IV–7), pp. 65–7; Wells (IV–23), pp. 276–8.

26 Pete Rowsome, site supervisor for Museum of London, quoted in *New Scientist*, 29 August 1985.

27 Clive. Thomas, *The Complete Works of Lord Macaulay*, 12 vols (1898), Vol. VII, p. 362.

Chapter 7: Eighty Thousand Dead

1 See Frere, Sheppard, *Verulamium Excavations*, Vol. I, Reports of the Research Committee of the Society of Antiquaries of London no. XXVIII (Oxford 1972); Webster (1–3), p. 124.

2 Tacitus (III–1), pp. 328–9; Dio (III–23), VIII, p. 95; Webster (1–3), p. 124.

3 Todd (II–8), p. 91 for ten thousand; Webster, Graham, *The Roman Imperial Army of the First and Second Centuries AD* (2nd edn reprinted with corrections 1981), p. 229 for 15,000–20,000.

4 See Fuentes, Nicholas, 'Boudicca re-visited', *London Archaeologist*, Vol. 4, no. 12 (1983); Webster, Graham, 'The Site of Boudica's Last Battle: A Comment', and Nicholas Fuentes' response to Graham Webster, *London Archaeologist*, Vol. 4, no. 15 (1984).

5 See Webster, 'The Site' (VII–4).

6 Spence, Lewis, *Boadicea: Warrior Queen of the Britons* (1937), p. 248.

7 See Fuentes (VII–4).

8 See *Transactions of the Birmingham Archaeological Society* (Oxford), Vol. 79 (1964), pp. 117–20 for Adrian Oswald on coins and an earthenwork from Mancetter; Vol. 84 (1971), pp. 18–44 for evidence of a first-century ditch; Vol. 85 (1973), pp. 211–13 for possible importance of the site in association with the great revolt of AD 60; Dudley and Webster (1–3), p. 111; Webster (1–3), p. 97 and fig. 5, p. 98. Other sources: Frere (IV–15), p. 107, 'reasonable guesses' have placed the site close to Watling Street, north-west of Towcester or near Mancetter; Salway (IV–7), p. 120: 'somewhere in the Midlands', Todd (II–8), p. 91: 'may not have been far to the north-west of Verulamium'.

9 Salway (IV–7), p. 77.

10 See Webster, *Army* (VII–3), pp. 122–32.

11 *The Tragedie of Bonduca* in *Comedies and Tragedies written by Francis Beaumont and John Fletcher, Gentlemen* . . . (1647), Act V, scene IV.

12 Bolton, Edmund, cit. Piggott (IV–9), p. 136; Jones, Inigo, *The Most Notable Antiquity of Great Britain, Vulgarly called Stone-Heng, on Salisbury Plain Restored* (2nd edn 1725), pp. 34–5.

13 Scott, J. M., *Boadicea* (1975), pp. 31f.; Spence (VII–5), p. 260; *The Times*, 23 February 1988; Nicholas fuentes, letter to *The Times*, 27 February 1988 thought Platform 8 – 'who knows' – not impossible.

14 Gibbon (1–9), 1, p. 39.

15 Tacitus, *Agricola* (IV–33), p. 67; Tacitus (III–1), p. 331; Bulst (V–2), p. 506; Overbeck (V–27), pp. 141–2.

16 Bulst (V–2), p. 506; Clarke (IV–9), p. 114.

17 Clarke (IV–9), p. 114; Bulst (V–2), p. 506 and note 80; Tacitus, *Agricola* (IV–33), p. 81.

18 Todd (II–8), p. 91; Salway (IV–7), Appendix IV, p. 751.

19 Cit. Nieng Cheng, *Life and Death in Shanghai* (1986), p. 203.

Chapter 8: O Zenobia!

1 *Historia Augusta* (V–5), III, p. 247; Dio (III–23), VIII, p. 83.

2 See Février, J. G., *Essai sur l'histoire politique et économique de Palmyre* (Paris 1931); Tlass, Moustapha, *Zénobie Reine de Palmyre: Oeuvre adaptée en français par Athanase Vantchev de Thracy* (Damascus 1986), *passim*.

3 I.e. Oliver Cromwell in seventeenth-century England, Fraser (VI–22), p. 564; Février, J. G., *La Religion des Palmyréniens* (Paris 1931), p. 222.

4 Cameron, Alan, 'The Date of Porphyry's KATA KRISTIANON', *Classical Quarterly*, XVII (1967), pp. 382–4.

5 *Historia Augusta* (V–5), III, p. 135.

6 See Abbott, Nabia, 'Pre-Islamic Arab Queens', *American Journal of Semitic Languages and Literature*, Vol. LVIII (1941), pp. 1–22.

7 Gibbon (1–9), I, p. 150.

8 Abbott, Nabia, 'Women and the State on the Eve of Islam', *American Journal of Semitic Languages and Literature*, Vol. LVIII (1941), pp. 269–78; Abbott, *Aishah* (1–11), p. x.

9 Abbott, 'Women' (VIII–8), p. 262; Beard, Mary R., *Women as Force in History: A Study in Traditions and Realities* (New York 1946), p. 290; Clayton, Ellen C., *Female Warriors: Memorials of Female Valour and Heroism, from the Mythological Ages to the Present Era*, 2 vols (1879), Vol. I, p. 88.

10 Février (VIII–2), pp. 59–62; Fedden, Robin, *Syria: An Historical Appreciation* (revised edn 1956), p. 87.

11 Février, *Religion* (VIII–3), p. 235.

12 *The History of Count Zosimus, Sometime Advocate and Chancellor of the Roman Empire* (1814), pp. 21f.; Février (VIII–2), p. 75.

13 Février (VIII–2), p. 85; *Historia Augusta* (V–5), III, p. 104 note 1.

14 See *Historia Augusta* (V–5), III, pp. 135f., but nothing is known of the various authors to whom the biographies are attributed: see *Oxford Companion to Classical Literature*, compiled by Sir Paul Harvey (Oxford 1984), p. 210.

15 *Historia Augusta* (V–5), III, pp. 135–43 for 'Trebellius Pollio's' description of Zenobia.

16 Gibbon (1–9), I, p. 302 and note 62; Boccaccio (1–19), p. 226; Jonson (1–2).

17 *Historia Augusta* (V–5), III, p. 109, for theory of Zenobia's conspiracy; Février (VIII–2), p. 90 believes in the possibility of Zenobia's guilt only because Herodianus' death helped her; a modern Arab writer, Moustapha Tlass (VIII–2), describes the accusations as 'gratuitous', since there is no proof of her complicity; Abbott, 'Queens' (VIII–6), p. 13 for Roman guilt.

18 *Historia Augusta* (V–5), III, p. 135; *Cambridge Ancient History*, Vol. XII (Cambridge 1939), p. 302.

19 Février, *Religion* (VIII–3), p. 241; *Cambridge Ancient History* (VIII–18), XII, p. 302.

20 Février (VIII–2), pp. 113–14; *Cambridge Ancient History* (VIII–18), XII, p. 302.

21 Février (VIII–2), p. 103.

22 Mommsen, Theodor, *The Provinces of the Roman Empire from Caesar to Diocletian*, Vol. II (1909), pp. 106–7 note 5.

23 Zosimus (VIII–12), p. 29.

24 Zosimus (VIII–12), pp. 25f.

25 *Historia Augusta* (v–5), III, pp. 243–4; Zosimus (VIII–12), p. 25.

26 Zosimus (VIII–12), p. 27; although the exchanges may well, of course, be fictional.

27 *Cambridge Ancient History* (VIII–18), XII, p. 306.

28 *Historia Augusta* (v–5), III, p. 137.

29 Zosimus (VIII–12), p. 29; *Historia Augusta* (v–5), III, p. 249.

30 Gibbon (1–9), I, pp. 311–12; *Historia Augusta* (v–5), III, pp. 141, 259; *Cambridge Ancient History* (VIII–18), XII, p. 305 note 1: 'Zosimus should be rejected'.

31 Perceval, A. P. Caussin de, *Essai sur l'histoire des Arabes avant l'Islamisme, pendant l'époque de Mahomet . . .*, Vol. II (Paris 1897), pp. 30 note 4, 192–8; Abbott, 'Queens' (VIII–6), p. 13.

32 Mommsen (VIII–22), p. 110; Gibbon (1–9), I, p. 308.

33 See Tlass (VIII–2), p. 169 note 1 for another Queen Al-Zabba, part of the royal family of Al-Hyra, sometimes confused with Zenobia.

34 *Zénobie* by Assi and Mansour Al-Rahbani, cit. Tlass (VIII–2), pp. 254–60.

35 *Zenobia: A Tragedy*, 'As it is performed at the Theatre Royal in Drury Lane. By the Author of the Orphan of China [Arthur Murphy]' (1768).

Index